Work-Life Balance

A Comprehensive Guide to Working Smarter, Not Harder. Strategies and Solutions for Gaining and Maintaining Balance

Elizabeth Bright

© **Copyright 2024 - All rights reserved.**

The content contained within this book may not be reproduced, duplicated or transmitted without direct written permission from the author or the publisher.

Under no circumstances will any blame or legal responsibility be held against the publisher, or author, for any damages, reparation, or monetary loss due to the information contained within this book, either directly or indirectly.

Legal Notice:

This book is copyright protected. It is only for personal use. You cannot amend, distribute, sell, use, quote or paraphrase any part, or the content within this book, without the consent of the author or publisher.

Disclaimer Notice:

Please note the information contained within this document is for educational and entertainment purposes only. All effort has been executed to present accurate, up to date, reliable, complete information. No warranties of any kind are declared or implied. Readers acknowledge that the author is not engaged in the rendering of legal, financial, medical or professional advice. The content within this book has been derived from various sources. Please consult a licensed professional before attempting any techniques outlined in this book.

By reading this document, the reader agrees that under no circumstances is the author responsible for any losses, direct or indirect, that are incurred as a result of the use of the information contained within this document, including, but not limited to, errors, omissions, or inaccuracies.

Table of Contents

DEDICATION 1

INTRODUCTION 3

CHAPTER 1: UNDERSTANDING WORK-LIFE BALANCE 7
   What Is Work-Life Balance? 8
      Pre-Industrial Revolution 8
      Industrial Revolution 9
      Early 20th Century 9
      Late 20th and Early 21st Century 9
   Benefits of Work-Life Balance 10
      Health and Well-Being 11
      Productivity and Performance 12
      Social and Personal Relationships 13
   Myths and Misconceptions 14
      All or Nothing Fallacy 14
      Career Sacrifice Myth 15
      One-Size-Fits-All Misconception 15
   The Consequences of Imbalance 16
      Physical Health 16
      Mental Well-Being 18
      Relationships 18
   Chapter Activity and Reflection Moment 19

CHAPTER 2: ASSESSING YOUR WORK-LIFE BALANCE 21
   Reflecting on Your Current Situation 22
      Assessment Questions 22
      Actions for Improvement 23
   Identifying Stressors and Imbalances 27
      Common Stressors 28
      Signs of Imbalance 29
      Actions for Improvement 30
   Assessing Satisfaction and Fulfillment 32
      Evaluating Satisfaction Levels 33
      Finding Fulfillment 35
      Actions for Improvement 37

CHAPTER ACTIVITY AND REFLECTION MOMENT 38
   Step 1: Identify Your Key Life Domains *38*
   Step 2: Draw Your Wheel *39*
   Step 3: Rate Your Satisfaction *39*
   Step 4: Color It In! *39*
   Step 5: Reflect and Analyze *39*
   Step 6: Set Goals for Improvement *40*
   Step 7: Review and Refine *40*

CHAPTER 3: STRATEGIES FOR ACHIEVING WORK-LIFE BALANCE 43

ALIGNING ACTIONS WITH HAPPINESS AND EXPECTATIONS 44
   Genuine Happiness Tasks *44*
   Obligatory Tasks *45*
   Expectation-Driven Tasks *45*
IDENTIFYING CORE VALUES 46
STRATEGIES FOR PRIORITIZING ACTIVITIES 47
   The Eisenhower Matrix *47*
   The Value vs. Complexity Matrix *49*
   The Pomodoro Method *51*
MASTERING TIME MANAGEMENT 52
   Prioritize and Delegate *53*
ESTABLISHING HEALTHY BOUNDARIES 56
   Work Boundaries *57*
   Family and Personal Relationship Boundaries *58*
CHAPTER ACTIVITY AND REFLECTION MOMENT 59

CHAPTER 4: NURTURING RELATIONSHIPS—GIVE YOURSELF AND OTHERS GRACE 61

THE IMPORTANCE OF HEALTHY RELATIONSHIPS 62
EMBRACING IMPERFECTIONS 63
BUILDING SUPPORTIVE RELATIONSHIPS 64
TOXIC VS. HEALTHY RELATIONSHIPS 65
   Signs of Toxic People *65*
   Signs of Healthy People *66*
CHAPTER ACTIVITY AND REFLECTION MOMENT 67
   Step 1: Reflect on Your Inner Circle *68*
   Step 2: Schedule Like You Mean It! *68*
   Step 3: Deepen The Connection *68*
   Step 4: Watch the Friendship Bloom *68*

CHAPTER 5: FLEXIBILITY AND ADAPTABILITY—EMBRACING CHANGE 71

UNDERSTANDING CHANGE 72
   Common Changes *72*

- Strategies for Embracing Change 74
  - Cultivate Curiosity and a Growth Mindset 74
  - Practice Self-Care and Build Resilience 75
  - Find Your Anchors and Celebrate Small Wins 75
- The Importance of Flexibility 75
  - Practice Saying Yes (And No) 76
  - Develop Multiple Solutions 76
  - Embrace Imperfection and Learn to Let Go 76
- Cultivating Adaptive Strategies 77
- Chapter Activity and Reflection Moment 78

CHAPTER 6: IMPACT ON YOUR MENTAL AND PHYSICAL HEALTH 81

- The Interplay of Work and Health 82
- Prioritizing Physical Health 83
- Prioritizing Mental Health 85
- Chapter Activity and Reflection Moment 86
  - Physical Health 86
  - Mental Health 87
  - Scoring 87

CHAPTER 7: WORK-LIFE BALANCE ACROSS DIFFERENT LIFE STAGES 89

- Early Career and Professional Development 90
- Parenting and Caregiving Responsibilities 91
- Empty Nesters and Retirement 93
- Chapter Activity and Reflection Moment 95
  - Reflect on Your Life Stage 95

CHAPTER 8: OVERCOMING COMMON BALANCE OBSTACLES 97

- Conquering Perfectionism 98
  - Overcoming Perfectionism 99
- Managing Fear of Failure 100
  - Overcoming Fear of Failure 101
- Societal Pressures 101
  - Overcoming Societal Pressures 102
- Chapter Activity and Reflection Moment 103

CHAPTER 9: MAINTAINING WORK-LIFE BALANCE LONG TERM BY CREATING BALANCE CULTURE 105

- Sustaining Work-Life Balance Over Time 106
  - Strategies for Sustainable Balance 106
- Creating a Work-Life Balance Culture 107
  - Employer Responsibility 108
  - Benefits of a Balanced Workplace 109
  - Side Effects of Unbalanced Work-Life Culture 110

 Chapter Activity and Reflection Moment 113

CHAPTER 10: WORK-LIFE BALANCE IN THE DIGITAL AGE—USING TECHNOLOGY TO YOUR ADVANTAGE **115**

 The Impact of Technology 116
 Leveraging Technology for Balance 117
  The reMarkable 2 Tablet *117*
  Oura Ring *119*
  ChatGPT *120*
 Digital Well-Being Practices 121
 Chapter Activity and Reflection Moment 122
  Part 1: A Digital Detox Audit *122*
  Part 2: Taming the Tech Tigers *123*
  Part 3: Your Digital Well-Being Manifesto *123*

CONCLUSION **125**

ABOUT THE AUTHOR **129**

REFERENCES **131**

Dedication

Dedicated to my husband, Jeff, who has supported me in every endeavor.

Dedicated to my three daughters, Jacqueline, Julia, and Lindy. You can have it all. You just need to define what that means to you and set goals to achieve it. Be ok with changing direction. Be ok with the definition changing. Winning is different for everyone. When I look back, there are things I would have changed, but then I think about what I have learned on the journey. I want you to learn and grow. I want you to make decisions and then change your mind because you learned. Life is an amazing journey.

Introduction

A group of young girls were recently asked what they wanted to be when they grew up. Very quickly, the group was divided into two groups: the corporate girlies, who were excited to be boss ladies and had thriving careers, and the homemakers, who expressed excitement to be moms and wives, bakers, and gardeners. At the end of the line sat little Susan, uncertain how to express her own answer. As the line got shorter and shorter, eventually, little Susan had to stand up and tell the class what she wanted to be when she grew up—her turn to pick a side. Filled with nervous energy and unsure what her friends would think of her, she bravely shared her answer. "I want to be an engineer," she said, "and a mom." The rest of the class grew quiet as they all stared at little Susan. "I want to do both," she proclaimed proudly. After a moment of silence, the other girls started changing their answers. "I also want both!" her friends chirped. "I didn't know that was an option," another shared. With great pride, Susan smiled, confirming to her friends that they could indeed have it all.

We're often trained to believe that we can only have one or the other. "Having it all" is simply a myth, a wonderful dream that can never be obtained. But is it really, or did little Susan perhaps have the courage to dream big enough for all of us? Well, let me tell you that it's entirely possible to have it all, but it's up to you to determine what that means to you. Having it all might mean something entirely different to you than it does to me, but it's not impossible. Imagine it as tending to a garden. The "perfect" garden for me would look different than your perfect garden, but it's possible for both gardens to thrive! With the right boundaries, strategies, and tools, we can have it all!

If you just read that and were tempted to throw this book across the room due to believing it's impossible, then you're in the right place! Perhaps you currently feel burned out from trying to juggle all the balls in your life, or maybe you feel like you're constantly neglecting one of the areas, either work or personal life. Regardless of your current situation, I want to encourage you and empower you to know that it's possible to balance work and life, even though it might not currently feel that way. On this journey, I'll share with you the insights and techniques that I've learned through years of personal experience and research, as well as the helpful tools I've acquired as a mentor, wife, mother, and leader. Let's have a quick look at all the topics we'll discuss on this journey to balance:

- In Chapter One, we'll explore the concept of work-life balance in depth, including its definition, benefits, and challenges. This includes exploring misconceptions and myths regarding work-life balance and the consequences of a poor work-life balance.

- Next, we'll assess our own work-life balance. I'll provide you with the right tools to assess your current work-life balance, creating the perfect starting block for moving forward on this journey.

- Once we've assessed our own work-life balance, we'll begin by exploring strategies for achieving a balance that will allow each and every one of us to have it all. This will include practical tips and managing stress and burnout.

- In Chapter Four, we'll dive into nurturing relationships by giving ourselves and those around us some grace for growth. We'll look at the importance of healthy relationships with family, friends, and colleagues, and I'll provide you with some tips to maintain strong relationships even when you're also focusing on your career goals.

- After that, we'll look at the importance of flexibility and adaptability and why we should be open to embracing change. We'll discuss certain strategies that will help us to find creative solutions to challenges in our lives.

- Later, we'll also discover the impact that poor balance can have on your mental and physical health and why it's essential to take care of yourself in order to have it all. We'll talk about cultivating meaning and fulfillment and how to live a life that is filled with healthy habits that contribute to your work-life balance and satisfaction.

- In Chapter Seven, we'll explore how work-life balance needs and priorities change over time, especially from the beginning of your career to retirement. We'll discuss advice for every stage, including for parents, caregivers, empty nesters, and retirees.

- Once we've discussed the different stages and how they might impact our work-life needs, we'll address common obstacles that you might face on your journey to true balance. Not only will we explore the obstacles, but we'll also discuss various practical tips and solutions to overcoming these obstacles and building resilience.

- In Chapter Nine, we'll take a look at maintaining the work-life balance we've worked so hard to achieve thus far. We want long-term change, which is why we need to discuss the strategies that will allow ongoing and constant assessment and adaptation.

- Finally, we'll end the journey by exploring how we can incorporate technology to make our work-life balance easier to achieve. Why fight the digital age when we can use it to improve our quality of life? We'll explore how to integrate it into our daily lives and how it can be beneficial for both our personal and professional lives.

Every chapter will consist of enlightening information, rich in knowledge and wisdom, along with personal stories, a section for self-reflection, and an encouraging activity to help you implement the knowledge into your life practically. If all of this seems like a lot to digest right now, take a deep breath and find confidence in the fact that you're not alone. I'll walk you through it every step of the way.

Now, you might be wondering, is work-life balance really this important? Should we really dedicate this much time, energy, and resources to finding the perfect work-life balance? Well, yes! According to a study conducted by the American Psychological Association, work-life balance is the second most important factor in job satisfaction, just behind a good salary (American Psychological Association, 2023). Yet, most of us struggle to prioritize our well-being and create boundaries to protect our professional and personal lives. Not anymore! My goal is to empower and equip you so that by the end of this book, you'll be confident in what you want and know how to achieve a work-life balance that will support your goals and dreams, allowing you to have it all.

Who am I to teach you all these wonderful things and make promises that seem so out of reach? Allow me to introduce myself. My name is Elizabeth, and I can confidently share with you that I have it all. Not only am I an author, senior vice president at a leading manufacturing company, and adjunct professor for master's degree courses on operations management, but I am also a devoted wife and mother of three. I've experienced the struggles of work-life balance personally, but with over three decades of experience in my career, I've found the balance that provides me with everything I want in life. On top of my career and my family life, I also have time to volunteer, serve on several boards of directors and advocacy groups, and support my kids from the side of the sports field. I fully believe in the power of self-care, personal growth, and finding joy in everyday moments, and that has led me to find a work-life balance that works for me.

So, are you ready to embark on this journey and discover your own work-life balance? Even though it might sound far-fetched, trust the process and know that anything is possible. Just like little Susan, you can have it all!

Chapter 1:

Understanding Work-Life Balance

Balance is not something you find, it's something you create. –Jana Kingsford

What do you consider work-life balance? What do you picture when you hear that you have the opportunity to achieve a healthy work-life balance? If you picture someone who is always on time, perfect in everything they do, and never drops a ball, you might have a slightly skewed perception of what balance is. Work-life balance doesn't mean being 100% present and on point in all the roles that you want to be in all the time. You're a real human being, after all, not Barbie. On the cover of this book, an old-school scale shows career on one side and family on the other. If you want to be a 100% career woman, there won't be any weights left to place on the other side of the scale, causing an imbalance and an empty personal life. However, the opposite is also true: If you place all the weights on the other side, you'll have nothing left for the career side. True balance happens when your time, devotion, and priority are allocated to different sides of the scale, depending on the needs of your current life.

Sometimes, more weight is needed on one side of the scale, and that's normal. You can borrow some weight from the different sides to ensure that you have enough time and energy to devote where it's needed. So, if you expected to magically clone yourself in order to give 100% at home and 100% at work at the same time, I have some bad news for you. But don't be discouraged. This idea of being perfect all the time isn't true balance, and in this chapter, we'll discover what work-life balance is. We'll also explore the benefits of achieving balance, the misconceptions regarding it, and the consequences of imbalance. So, get ready to move around some weights on your scale of life as we begin to understand work-life balance better.

What Is Work-Life Balance?

Work-life balance goes beyond a simple time-management equation. It's the art of cultivating a fulfilling and sustainable existence where your professional obligations and personal aspirations coexist harmoniously (Borowiec & Drygas, 2023). This ideal state isn't about dividing your hours equally between work and everything else. The core principle lies in ensuring that neither aspect of your life encroaches excessively on the other. While work is undoubtedly important, it shouldn't leave you depleted of energy or prevent you from engaging in activities that bring you joy and a sense of well-being outside of your career.

What makes the concept of work-life balance a little tricky is the fact that the specific makeup of a healthy work-life balance is unique to each individual. It depends on your personal priorities, stage of life, and overall goals. For some, it might involve dedicating time to hobbies and passions, while others might prioritize spending quality time with family or friends. The key is to find a rhythm that allows you to thrive in both your professional and personal spheres. Ideally, work should energize you and provide a sense of accomplishment, while your personal life offers a space to unwind, recharge, and pursue your passions. This balanced approach can lead to a more fulfilling and sustainable life in the long run.

Over the years, the concept of work-life balance has changed and evolved significantly, and it has a surprisingly complex history. Let's take a closer look at how the idea evolved over time.

Pre-Industrial Revolution

Before the 18th century, work and life weren't different spheres but rather blended together (Hornsby, 2022). Farming, artisanal crafts, and domestic chores were intertwined, with long hours being the norm. People also had very little leisure time as survival and subsistence often dictated daily activities. Back then, societal roles played a huge part, and work was often defined by gender and social class. Men focused on physical labor, while women managed the home and raised the children.

Industrial Revolution

During the 18th and 19th centuries, the rise of factories occurred. The factory system separated work from home, creating the first clear division between work hours and personal house. However, the work hours were very long, as the factory workers often endured grueling schedules, exceeding 10-12 hours a day, six days a week (Striking Women, 2013). This created the need for labor movements. As the working conditions worsened, labor movements emerged to fight for shorter workweeks and safer environments. This created the start of the five-day workweek (*The Progressive Era*, n.d.).

Early 20th Century

The concept of an eight-hour workday gained traction during the early 20th century, pioneered by reformers. With shorter workweeks, leisure time became a possibility for some, which led to the development of new industries, such as entertainment and tourism (Baron, 2015). During this period, we also saw a great gender shift as more and more women entered the workforce, adding another layer to the work-life balance discussion. Even as women entered the workforce, it was still expected of them to manage traditional roles, such as homemaking and raising children.

Late 20th and Early 21st Century

With the rise of technology, work has been made accessible 24/7, once again blurring the work-life boundaries as before (Ljungkvist & Moore, 2023). However, this also created the need for work-life balance, and focusing more on family activities became a goal for many. Having healthy boundaries is considered essential, and most workers understand the need for it. Companies have also started offering flexible work schedules and remote work options in order to help employees achieve work-life balance within a customized space that works for them (Ljungkvist & Moore, 2023).

As we look to the future, we can assume that the concept will continue to evolve along with the generations and societal values. Currently, there's a growing emphasis on overall well-being, with work being seen as just one aspect of a fulfilling life. As technology continues to advance, the very nature of work and how it integrates into our lives is likely to transform in unexpected ways, and, therefore, we can assume that the definition will continue to evolve, just as we do.

Now that we have a better understanding of the real definition of work-life balance, we should probably consider why it's so important. If it's become a goal for many, surely it must have some benefits. Let's have a closer look!

Benefits of Work-Life Balance

Of course, work-life balance has many benefits; otherwise, me writing this book and you currently reading it would be an absolute waste of time. But for many, it's a little bit like taking vitamins: We know it's good for us but don't necessarily take them. In the same way, we understand that work-life balance is important and that it's beneficial, but do we really understand why? There might be more reasons than what you think at this moment. They go way beyond just the obvious, so let's explore the benefits categorized into three groups:

- health and well-being benefits
- productivity and performance benefits
- social and personal relationships benefits

Remember, this isn't one of those "too good to be true" moments. You can have it all, including all of these incredible benefits.

Health and Well-Being

First of all, let me say that work-life balance isn't just a trendy buzzword but a crucial factor for maintaining good physical and mental health. When you can effectively divide your time and energy between professional demands and personal well-being, you reap a multitude of benefits. When it comes to physical health, a healthy work-life balance can help reduce stress. Chronic work stress can lead to a cascade of physical problems, including high blood pressure, heart disease, and weakened immune function. A healthy work-life balance allows you to de-stress, lowering your risk of these conditions. It also improves your sleep, which is vital for physical repair and cognitive function. When you're constantly plugged into work, disconnecting and getting enough sleep becomes difficult. Work-life balance allows for proper sleep hygiene, promoting overall physical health. A proper work-life balance can also lead to healthier habits. Having dedicated personal time allows you to prioritize healthy habits like exercising and preparing nutritious meals. These habits improve your physical well-being and energy levels (Motion Blog, 2023).

When we look at the benefits to your mental health, they're equally important. A healthy work-life balance can help reduce anxiety. Working constantly can cause a lot of anxiety, which can lead to even more mental health issues (Motion Blog, 2023). Disconnecting from work allows you to manage worries, improving your overall mental well-being. It also contributes to overall increased happiness. When you have time for activities you enjoy and that bring you a sense of fulfillment, your happiness levels increase. This positive emotional state has a ripple effect on your mental health.

Overall, work-life balance promotes a holistic approach to health. By addressing both your physical and mental needs, you create a foundation for a more fulfilling and resilient life. You'll have the energy and focus to tackle challenges at work and enjoy your personal life to the fullest.

Productivity and Performance

Another major benefit of work-life balance is its ability to promote your productivity and performance. Achieving work-life balance isn't just about feeling good outside of work; it significantly contributes to your success within it. It fosters job satisfaction, engagement, and effectiveness.

A solid work-life balance can reduce the chances of burnout in terms of job satisfaction. When work bleeds into every aspect of your life, it can lead to feelings of exhaustion and resentment (Motion Blog, 2023). Work-life balance prevents burnout, allowing you to find fulfillment and enjoyment in your job. Having dedicated personal time allows you to recharge and return to work feeling refreshed and motivated, which can also lead to a greater sense of accomplishment as you tackle tasks with renewed energy. Finding balance doesn't mean complete separation. When you can integrate work and personal life in a healthy way (e.g., flexible schedules, remote work options), it can decrease stress and increase overall satisfaction.

Work-life balance also increases engagement. When you feel well-rested and have time for personal pursuits, your ability to focus and maintain clarity during work hours will increase. This leads to deeper engagement with your tasks. You're also more likely to be proactive and contribute meaningful ideas when feeling energetic and engaged, which is why having a fulfilling personal life boosts overall motivation and initiative (Wedgwood, 2022). Work-life balance also promotes a more positive work environment. Employees experiencing less stress are more likely to collaborate effectively, leading to a more harmonious and productive team dynamic.

Work-life balance has a great effect on your effectiveness at work. Since chronic stress can cloud your judgment, a clear mind achieved through work-life balance will help you make better decisions, solve problems more creatively, and approach tasks with a strategic mindset. Time away from work allows your mind to wander and creativity to flourish, which can lead to innovative solutions and fresh perspectives on work challenges. Work-life balance can also increase your productivity. Employees who are well-rested, motivated, and focused tend to be more productive. Work-life balance allows you to work smarter, not just harder, leading to higher-quality output in less time.

One example of this can be seen in Toyota's flexible work arrangements. Toyota, one of the leading car manufacturers in the world, offers various flexible work arrangements for their employees. They can choose to telecommute and even have access to compressed workweeks. These arrangements were originally put in place to enhance employee well-being, but the results also showed an increase in work productivity. Not only do the employees have higher satisfaction, higher morale, and lower stress levels, but they actually work more productively and get more work done than they did in traditional environments (Smith, 2020).

Social and Personal Relationships

The final category of benefits that work-life balance has in store for us is healthy social and personal relationships. The truth is, work-life balance isn't just about you. It also positively (or negatively) impacts the people around you and your overall happiness. First of all, it affects your family dynamics. When you're not constantly consumed by work, you have more quality time to dedicate to your family, which strengthens bonds, fosters communication, and creates lasting memories. It also helps you to be more present and patient with your family, as you'll be less stressed and therefore less irritable. By maintaining a healthy work-life balance, you also set a positive example for your family members, encouraging them to value a healthy work-life balance for themselves.

Work-life balance will also affect your friendships. When work consumes all your time, friends can feel neglected or resentful. Work-life balance allows you to dedicate time to friendships, as you can schedule outings, maintain regular communication, and strengthen your social support network. By doing so, you will spend more quality time with friends and foster shared experiences, creating lasting memories and a sense of belonging.

As you can see, work-life balance isn't just about achieving personal well-being; it creates a ripple effect that positively impacts your family dynamics, friendships, and overall happiness. By prioritizing a healthy work-life balance, you invest not only in yourself but also in the well-being of those around you. You create a more fulfilling life for yourself and contribute to stronger, happier relationships. Now that we actually understand the benefits of a balanced work-life, it's time to take a look at common myths and misconceptions.

Myths and Misconceptions

Myths and misconceptions are false beliefs that are often accepted as true. They can arise from various sources, like folklore, outdated information, or simply misunderstandings. These mistaken ideas can spread easily through word-of-mouth or even media portrayals. There are many myths and misconceptions regarding a healthy work-life balance, but it's time we look to the truth and not just what everyone believes blindly. There are three specific myths and misconceptions I want to focus on, so let's get right to it.

All or Nothing Fallacy

The all-or-nothing fallacy is a cognitive bias that leads us to believe things can only exist in extremes. In the context of work-life balance, it manifests as the misconception that achieving balance requires a perfect 50/50 split between work and personal life or that any deviation from that is a failure (Deal, 2022). However, that's not true, and here's why I say so.

First of all, life is fluid. Our lives aren't static but dynamic; work demands might fluctuate week to week, and personal needs can change, too. A healthy balance is about adapting and prioritizing based on current circumstances. Balance also doesn't mean equal time. There's no magic formula for work-life balance; it's not about rigidly dividing time equally. Some days, work might require more attention, while others might be more personal life- focused, which is why this is a myth and not the truth. On top of all of that, work-life balance isn't about perfection but about progress. It involves conscious effort and ongoing adjustments, which is why it can't be an all-or-nothing approach. By letting go of the all-or-nothing fallacy, you can create a sustainable and fulfilling work-life balance that works for you.

Career Sacrifice Myth

The "career sacrifice myth" suggests that achieving work-life balance necessitates giving up on your career aspirations. This misconception can prevent you from prioritizing well-being, ultimately hindering your personal and professional life (Myers, 2017). Here's why it's a myth.

When you're well-rested and have time for activities that energize you, you approach work with greater focus and clarity. This can actually lead to increased productivity and a better quality of work, not a decrease. Taking breaks and allowing your mind to wander can spark creativity. A healthy work-life balance allows for this mental space, potentially leading to innovative ideas and problem-solving approaches (Myers, 2017). Chronic stress from work overload can cloud judgment. Work-life balance promotes clear thinking, allowing you to make better decisions that benefit your career in the long run.

The bottom line is that work-life balance isn't a concession; it's an investment in your career success. By prioritizing your well-being, you'll be a more focused, creative, and effective employee. This not only benefits your personal life but also paves the way for long-term career growth and satisfaction.

One-Size-Fits-All Misconception

The idea that there's a universal recipe for work-life balance is a tempting but ultimately misleading notion. While everyone strives for a healthy blend of professional and personal fulfillment, the path to achieving it is as individual as we are. Consider the introvert who flourishes after a focused workday and craves quiet evenings to recharge versus the extrovert who gains energy from social interaction and might find integrating work with evening gatherings more enriching—the same "balance" won't work for both of these individuals. Our family dynamics also play a large role, since a single parent might prioritize flexible work arrangements to accommodate childcare needs, while someone with a stay-at-home spouse might seek a clear separation between work hours and family time. The key lies in recognizing and respecting these differences when seeking your own balance.

There's no magic formula—the ideal balance is the one that allows you to be your most engaged and fulfilled self, both at work and in your personal life. This might involve setting boundaries, experimenting with flexible schedules, or simply prioritizing activities that energize you outside of the office. By embracing individual needs and preferences, we can move away from a one-size-fits-all approach and craft a work-life balance that fosters genuine well-being.

By busting these myths, we can better understand what work-life balance really means. But in order to get a truly accurate picture, we also need to look at the opposite of work-life balance and the consequences of imbalance.

The Consequences of Imbalance

If work-life balance can offer so many wonderful things in our lives, then surely the opposite is also true, right? Absolutely! What many don't realize is serious consequences result from work-life imbalance, as it can affect our physical health, mental well-being, relationships, and general quality of life.

Physical Health

The first way that our physical health gets impacted by work-life imbalance is that it increases stress. When work demands become overwhelming and constantly intrude on personal time, the body goes into fight-or-flight mode (Eludinni, 2016).

This triggers the release of stress hormones like cortisol, which can:

- increase blood pressure and heart rate
- suppress the immune system
- contribute to weight gain by increasing cravings for sugary and fatty foods
- lead to muscle tension and headaches

Not only can it contribute to stress, but it can also lead to constantly feeling fatigued. Since sleep is crucial for physical health and mental rejuvenation, you will begin to feel fatigued when you don't get enough quality sleep. Eventually, the fatigue can lead to (Eludinni, 2016):

- decreased concentration and productivity
- increased risk of accidents and injuries
- weakened immune system
- mood swings and irritability

Finally, work-life imbalance can also affect your physical health by making you more susceptible to illness. Chronic stress and fatigue take a toll on the immune system, making you more susceptible to (Eludinni, 2016):

- colds and flu
- infections
- autoimmune diseases
- chronic health conditions like heart disease and diabetes

Long story short, by prioritizing a healthy work-life balance, you can manage stress levels, improve sleep quality, and strengthen your immune system, all of which contribute to better overall physical health.

Mental Well-Being

Work-life imbalance isn't just about feeling physically drained; it can have a profound impact on your mental well-being. When the boundaries between work and personal life blur, constant pressure and a sense of never being "off" can lead to a cascade of mental health issues. Chronic stress fuels anxiety, making you feel on edge and worried even outside of work hours. This constant state of worry can disrupt sleep patterns, further exacerbating feelings of anxiety and exhaustion. Over time, the emotional toll of work overload can contribute to depression, characterized by feelings of hopelessness, low motivation, and a loss of interest in activities you once enjoyed (Borowiec & Drygas, 2023).

Perhaps the most significant risk of work-life imbalance is burnout. Burnout is a state of emotional, physical, and mental exhaustion caused by prolonged or excessive stress, and it can manifest as cynicism, detachment from work, and a sense of reduced accomplishment, further impacting self-esteem and overall mental well-being. By creating a healthier work-life balance, you can manage stress, improve sleep quality, and foster a sense of control, all essential for safeguarding your mental health.

Relationships

In the same way that a healthy work-life balance can also affect your friends, family, and colleagues, an imbalance can do the same. When work consistently bleeds into personal time, it can create significant strain on both personal and professional relationships. Spouses, partners, and children often feel neglected and resentful when work demands take priority over quality time together (Tomazevic et al., 2014). This can lead to arguments, a lack of emotional connection, and, ultimately, a weakened family unit. Friendships can also suffer as constant work commitments make it difficult to maintain social connections.

Feeling constantly stressed and overwhelmed can make you withdrawn and less engaged with others, leading to feelings of isolation and loneliness. Professionally, work-life imbalance can also be detrimental. Being constantly burnt out can lead to decreased productivity, missed deadlines, and increased errors. Additionally, a stressed and irritable demeanor can create tension with colleagues and supervisors. Ultimately, a lack of work-life balance can leave you feeling dissatisfied in both your personal and professional spheres (Tomazevic et al., 2014).

So, what does all of this mean? Let's summarize. Work-life imbalance isn't just about feeling squeezed; it chips away at the very foundations of a fulfilling life. When work constantly intrudes on personal time, it becomes difficult to nurture the relationships, hobbies, and activities that bring us joy. Chronic stress and exhaustion leave us emotionally drained, with little energy left for the things that truly matter. This lack of engagement with the things we value leads to feelings of dissatisfaction and a sense that life is passing us by. Ultimately, work-life imbalance undermines our ability to experience true happiness and fulfillment, leaving us feeling like we're just going through the motions rather than actively creating a life we love.

As we reach the end of our first chapter together, let's take a moment for self-reflection and use the opportunity to create actionable steps based on what we've learned in this chapter. In the next chapter, we'll assess our current work-life balance, which will set us up for the rest of the journey ahead.

Chapter Activity and Reflection Moment

Take a moment to reflect and journal on these questions.

- What does an ideal work-life balance look like to me personally?
- Why is a balanced work-life important to me?
- Am I currently showcasing any signs of imbalance?

After you've journaled, consider your current work-life balance. You don't have to assess it too deeply just yet, since that's what Chapter 2 is all about, but allow your mind to notice moments where you are showcasing signs of imbalance. Allowing yourself to notice these small things will help you in the next chapter, where we'll begin to actively assess and change our work-life balance for the better.

Chapter 2:

Assessing Your Work-Life Balance

Happiness is not a matter of intensity but of balance, order, rhythm, and harmony.

–Thomas Merton

Early in my career, when I had a very young family, I often overcommitted to activities. I thought that *having* it all meant *doing* it all. As others applauded me for doing everything and being a "wonder woman," I felt proud and wore it like a badge of honor. I honestly believed that all the other women in my life were committing to the same things I was, doing it all and looking good while doing so. So, I felt this intense pressure to do even more and be even better. I had to be the best at my job, have a happy family, spend quality time with friends, maintain a spotless home without asking for help, volunteer, work overtime, travel, have more babies, attend every school event, and never, ever drop the ball. You name it, and I was committed to doing it. I was convinced that it was expected of me, so I would get up at 5 a.m. and go to bed after midnight. At first, it seemed manageable, but over time, it began to impact my physical and mental health. Yet, if you asked me at that time whether I believed I was living a balanced life, I would've said yes. It was only later in life that I realized having it all didn't mean doing it all.

In this chapter, we'll have the opportunity to assess our own work-life balance. As you can see from this story I just shared, sometimes we think that we live a balanced life, even when that's not the case. So, keep an open mind as you begin this assessment. Be honest with yourself as you're answering these questions and reflecting on your own life. However, do it with kindness toward yourself. Don't judge yourself for neglecting certain areas or for feeling inadequate. The goal isn't to judge yourself harshly but to accurately assess your work-life balance so that you'll know what to work on next. Let's start it off by reflecting on our current situations.

Reflecting on Your Current Situation

Accurately assessing your work-life balance requires honest reflection of your current situation. Just like fingerprints, our ideal balance is unique. By reflecting on our energy levels, emotional state, and how much time we dedicate to different areas of life, we can identify areas of imbalance. Are we constantly exhausted? Do we neglect our hobbies and social connections? These signals help us understand how work demands are impacting our overall well-being and pave the way for creating a balance that fosters genuine fulfillment. Let's start off by asking ourselves a few assessment questions. Remember, no one else will see this, so you can be brutally honest with yourself.

Assessment Questions

Take your time to answer the following questions. You can answer them mentally, but I recommend using a journal. That way, you can always come back and look at the progress you've made along the way. I have also created a Companion Workbook to use along with this book, so be sure to keep that nearby. Give yourself a score out of five for every question (1 = Terrible/Never; 2 = Sometimes; 3 = Fifty-Fifty/Neutral; 4 = Mostly positive; 5 = Excellent/Always).

1. Do you currently feel good about the balance between your work and personal life?

2. Do you consider yourself in balance right now?

3. Do you know how to maintain a work-life balance?

4. How often are you on time for work-related appointments and never run late?

5. How often are you on time for personal appointments and never run late?

6. Do you feel fulfilled and satisfied in your working life?

7. How good are you at prioritizing your time between work, family, hobbies, and personal well-being?

8. Do you have support in your life to ensure you achieve your goals?

9. You always balance your work life so that you don't overcommit yourself.

10. Do you find it easy to say no?

Calculate your score out of 50. If you have less than 25, that's a clear indicator that you need improvement in your work-life balance. Anything below 45 can also be seen as a slight warning sign, even though things might not be out of hand yet. If you have a near-perfect score, well done, but stick around; you might still learn a thing or two.

Actions for Improvement

Based on your answers, it's time to take some action and make some improvements, don't you think? Even if your answers didn't reveal that you're completely out of balance, there is always room for improvement. So, with that in mind, here are three actions you can take to improve on your current situation based on the assessment questions.

Activities That Bring Joy

The first way to improve your current situation is to start by prioritizing activities that bring you joy, not the activities that you feel you need to get done. Prioritizing activities can help you reduce stress in your life and improve your overall well-being. Engaging in enjoyable activities will help you to unwind, de-stress, and recharge, leading to increased energy levels and a more positive outlook on life (Venkat, 2022). It also boosts your creativity and problem-solving skills, benefiting your personal and work life.

Here are some ideas to get you started on finding activities that bring you joy and fulfillment:

- **Pursue a creative outlet:** Writing, painting, playing music, or engaging in any form of artistic expression can be incredibly rewarding.

- **Connect with nature:** Hiking, gardening, or simply spending time outdoors can be great ways to de-stress and appreciate nature's beauty.

- **Learn a new skill:** Take a cooking class, learn a language, or start coding. The possibilities are endless!

- **Volunteer your time:** Giving back to your community can be a meaningful way to spend your time and connect with others.

- **Travel and explore:** Whether it's a weekend getaway or a long-awaited adventure, travel can broaden your horizons and create lasting memories.

- **Spend time with loved ones:** Nurture your relationships with family and friends through shared activities and quality time.

- **Reflect on what you like to do:** Take time to really consider the things that you want to do in life and the things that bring you joy.

Setting Boundaries

Setting boundaries is a crucial action for achieving work-life balance, and it's probably one of the main reasons your current assessment might not have looked so great. Boundaries are all about establishing clear lines between your work and personal life to ensure you have dedicated time and energy for both (Elazab, 2023).

Here are some examples of how to set boundaries:

- **Communicate your work hours:** Clearly define your start and end times and stick to them as much as possible. Let colleagues know you won't be checking emails or responding to calls outside of these hours.

- **Turn off work notifications:** Don't let work notifications disrupt your personal time. Silence notifications on your phone and resist the urge to check work emails after hours.

- **Schedule dedicated "me-time":** Block out time in your calendar for activities you enjoy, whether it's exercising, spending time with loved ones, or simply relaxing. Treat these appointments as seriously as you would any work meeting.

- **Learn to say "no":** Don't be afraid to politely decline additional work tasks or requests that would interfere with your personal time. It's okay to prioritize your well-being.

Setting boundaries takes practice and assertiveness, but the benefits for work-life balance and overall well-being are significant. By establishing clear lines and sticking to them, you can create a more sustainable and fulfilling work-life experience (Elazab, 2023). Let's take a quick moment to reflect on our current boundaries.

Take a deep breath and consider these areas of your life:

- **Physical space:** Do you feel comfortable in your own home? Do other people's habits encroach on your space?

- **Time:** Are you constantly stretched thin? Do you ever feel like there just aren't enough hours in the day for what matters to you?

- **Emotions:** Do you find yourself drained by other people's negativity? Do you feel pressured to take on other people's burdens?

- **Information:** Does work bleed into your personal life? Do you feel obligated to be reachable 24/7?

- **Relationships:** Do you feel like you're constantly giving to others without getting anything back? Do some people in your life make you feel disrespected or uncomfortable?

Think about a recent situation where you wished you had a boundary in place. What did it look like? How would having a boundary have changed the outcome? By reflecting on these areas, you can start to identify where boundaries might be most needed. Remember, boundaries are about protecting your well-being, and they are essential for healthy relationships.

Delegate

Delegating isn't easy, especially if you're a bit of a control freak (guilty as charged). But delegating is essential if you want to find a healthy work-life balance. Delegating tasks and seeking support are powerful tools in your work-life balance toolbox. When your workload feels overwhelming, these strategies can help you free up time and energy for both your professional duties and personal life. Here are some actionable steps to help you delegate:

- **Identify delegable tasks:** Not everything needs to be done by you. Look for tasks that can be effectively handled by work colleagues, friends, family, and hired workers (in your personal life) who have the appropriate skills and experience. This could include administrative work, data entry, research, school pick-ups, or home cleaning.

- **Choose the right person:** Match the task to the skillset. Consider who on your team, both personally and professionally, has the capacity and expertise to complete the delegated task successfully. You might hire a professional cleaner or ask a friend who loves driving around to pick up that birthday cake you ordered across town.

- **Provide clear instructions:** Don't set someone up for failure. Clearly explain the task, desired outcome, and deadlines. Be open to questions and provide any necessary resources. Don't just tell your partner to go grocery shopping; express to them when you would like it to be finished and what your expectations are.

- **Empower your team:** Trust your colleagues and the people in your personal life to take ownership of the delegated task. This doesn't mean micromanaging. Instead, give them the space to use their skills and judgment.

- **Recognize and appreciate:** Acknowledge a job well done. Thanking your colleagues and the people in your life (even if you're paying them) for their contributions fosters a positive environment and encourages future delegation.

Remember, delegation and seeking support aren't signs of weakness; they're signs of intelligence and effective leadership. By leveraging the skills and resources around you, you can achieve more, reduce stress, and create a more manageable work-life balance. It's also essential to know that delegating isn't always the answer. Sometimes, you can just accept the dirty kitchen as is without asking someone to clean it immediately. Some things can wait for tomorrow while you enjoy your me-time or family time.

Identifying Stressors and Imbalances

Well done, you've accomplished step one in your self-assessment. Up next, we'll move toward identifying stressors and imbalances in our lives. Since I can't personally take a look at your life and tell you which areas are adding stress, you'll have to dig a little deeper into your own life and try to view things from an objective view. It's always easier to see the issues in other people's lives, isn't it? So, let's pretend we're watching a movie where we are the main characters. Can you spot the imbalance now? Well, perhaps these common stressors will help you or at least point you in the right direction.

Common Stressors

Many things can cause us to be stressed. These common stressors are often the root of many other stressors in our lives, which is why it's so important to identify them. Let's take a closer look at some of the most common stressors.

Lack of Boundaries Between Work and Personal Life

This is a major roadblock to achieving work-life balance. When the line between work and personal time blurs, it can get tricky to see clearly what needs to be done and by when. Imagine checking work emails or fielding calls during evenings and weekends or feeling pressured to be available at all times. The fact that we all have our phones glued to our hands also makes it easy to allow work lines to get blurred. This constant connectivity creates a sense of never being truly "off the clock," bleeding work stress into your personal life and making it nearly impossible to relax and de-stress. This can be quite harmful since employees are much more productive when they take care of themselves and set boundaries to de-stress (Gudhka, 2023).

Long Working Hours

This is a common and significant stressor. When you're constantly putting in long hours or struggling to manage an overloaded schedule, it can be difficult to find time for anything else—personal relationships, hobbies, or even basic self-care go by the wayside. This chronic imbalance can lead to exhaustion, decreased productivity (due to fatigue and stress), and, eventually, burnout. Feeling perpetually behind and overwhelmed by work can negatively impact your mental and physical well-being, creating a vicious cycle that's difficult to escape. The constant strain can lead to anxiety and depression, creating a domino effect that weakens your immune system, putting you at a higher risk for chronic diseases like heart disease and stroke. With long working hours, you might also find yourself neglecting healthy habits like exercise and home-cooked meals, further impacting your well-being (Wong et al., 2019).

Neglect of Self-Care

Taking care of yourself, both physically and mentally, is essential for maintaining a healthy work-life balance. When you consistently neglect activities that bring you joy and relaxation, you become more susceptible to burnout and sickness (Getchius, 2019). This could involve skipping workouts, putting hobbies on hold indefinitely, or failing to schedule any dedicated downtime for relaxation. Without these outlets to relieve stress and recharge your batteries, work demands become overwhelming, leading to decreased energy, increased frustration, and, ultimately, a diminished ability to perform well at work (Getchius, 2019).

Signs of Imbalance

In addition to using these common culprits as indicators, we can also use the following signs of imbalance to guide us toward the things causing us stress.

Feeling Constantly Overwhelmed or Exhausted

This is a classic sign of work-life imbalance. When your work demands consistently exceed your capacity to cope, you feel constantly under pressure. You might find yourself struggling to prioritize tasks, feeling like there's never enough time, and constantly playing catch-up. This overload can lead to mental and physical exhaustion, making it difficult to concentrate, stay motivated, or simply function at your best.

Struggling to Meet Personal or Family Commitments due to Work Demands

This is a red flag that work is bleeding into your personal life in a negative way. If you're constantly late or missing important events, canceling plans with loved ones, or neglecting your responsibilities at home because of work, it's a clear sign that your work-life balance is out of whack. Work is important, but so are your personal relationships and well-being.

Experiencing Physical Symptoms of Stress

Our bodies often communicate stress through physical symptoms. When you're constantly stressed due to work-life imbalance, you might experience headaches, muscle tension, stomachaches, or difficulty sleeping (insomnia). These physical manifestations can further exacerbate the problem, creating a cycle of stress, exhaustion, and decreased productivity. If you're noticing a rise in unexplained physical ailments, it's crucial to consider whether your work-life balance might be contributing to the problem.

Actions for Improvement

Now, let's get down to business with a personal stress audit. This self-assessment is designed to help you identify your personal stress triggers and stressors. By reflecting on your experiences and habits, you can gain valuable insight into what throws you off balance and develop strategies to manage it.

Part 1: Daily Life

- **Typical day:** Briefly describe your daily routine, including work schedule, commute, and typical evening/weekend activities.

- **Work demands:** What aspects of your work do you find most stressful? (e.g., workload, deadlines, communication issues, lack of control)

- **Personal demands:** What personal commitments or responsibilities cause you stress (e.g., family obligations, finances, health concerns)?

- **Relaxation habits:** How often do you engage in activities that help you relax and de-stress (e.g., exercise, hobbies, spending time with loved ones)?

- **Sleep hygiene:** Do you have a regular sleep schedule? Do you experience difficulty falling asleep or staying asleep?

- **Social support:** How often do you connect with friends and family? Do you feel you have a strong support system?

Part 2: Stress Response

- **Physical symptoms:** Do you experience any physical symptoms when you're stressed (e.g., headaches, stomachaches, muscle tension, fatigue)?

- **Emotional signs:** How do you typically feel when you're stressed (e.g., overwhelmed, anxious, irritable, depressed)?

- **Behavioral changes:** Do you notice any changes in your behavior when you're stressed? (e.g., procrastination, overeating, social withdrawal)

Part 3: Triggers and Areas for Improvement

- **Identifying triggers:** Reflecting on your answers, are there any specific situations, people, or events that tend to trigger stress for you?

- **Areas for improvement:** Based on your responses, what areas of your life do you think could benefit from less stress? How can you implement that into your daily life?

Once you've completed this self-assessment, take some time to analyze your answers. Look for patterns and recurring themes. This will help you pinpoint the specific stressors and triggers that are most impactful in your life. With this newfound awareness, you can start to develop a personalized toolbox of strategies to manage stress and achieve a better work-life balance. Remember, it's essential to be honest with yourself and remember that this is an ongoing process. As your life circumstances change, so too may your stressors and coping mechanisms. Regularly revisit this audit or create a stress management plan to adapt and maintain your well-being.

Assessing Satisfaction and Fulfillment

Feeling satisfied and fulfilled are related but distinct concepts that contribute to overall well-being, both of which are essential when you want to live a full and happy life. Satisfaction is often described as a feeling of contentment or gratification. It's the sense of having a need, desire, or expectation met. Satisfaction can be temporary, arising from specific experiences or achievements. For example, you might feel satisfied after completing a challenging task at work, enjoying a delicious meal, or spending quality time with loved ones. Fulfillment, on the other hand, refers to a deeper sense of purpose, meaning, and overall contentment in life. It's the feeling that your life has value and your actions contribute to something bigger than yourself. Fulfillment is a more enduring state and isn't solely dependent on achieving specific goals. For example, you might feel fulfilled if your work allows you to use your talents and make a positive impact or if your relationships provide a deep sense of connection and love.

Imagine satisfaction as enjoying a delicious slice of cake. It brings temporary pleasure. Fulfillment, however, is like tending to a garden and watching it flourish over time. It's a more enduring and meaningful experience. When you have a balanced work-life situation, you will feel both satisfied and fulfilled. If you are looking for ways to be happier, I would encourage you to read my book, *Happy Habits*. In the book, it provides actions and activities that support improving your baseline happiness levels, and a part of that is feeling more satisfied and fulfilled.

Evaluating Satisfaction Levels

This quick quiz is designed to help you evaluate your current level of satisfaction in various aspects of life. There are no right or wrong answers, so be honest with yourself and choose the response that best reflects your current feelings. For each question, rate your satisfaction level on the following scale:

- Very Satisfied (5 points)
- Satisfied (4 points)
- Neutral (3 points)
- Dissatisfied (2 points)
- Very Dissatisfied (1 point)

Career

1. I feel fulfilled and challenged by my current work.
2. I have a good work-life balance, and my job rarely interferes with my personal time.
3. I feel valued and appreciated by my colleagues and superiors.
4. My current career path aligns with my long-term goals and aspirations.
5. I feel optimistic about the future of my career.

Relationships

1. I feel supported and loved by my close friends and family.
2. I have healthy and fulfilling relationships in my life.

3. I feel comfortable expressing myself openly and honestly with the people I care about.

4. I make time for the important relationships in my life, even when I'm busy.

5. My relationships contribute to my overall sense of well-being.

Health

1. I prioritize my physical and mental health by eating well, exercising regularly, and getting enough sleep.

2. I feel energized and have the stamina to tackle daily tasks.

3. I manage stress effectively and rarely feel overwhelmed.

4. I make time for relaxation and activities that promote inner peace.

5. I feel confident in my ability to cope with life's challenges.

Leisure

1. I have hobbies and interests that I enjoy pursuing outside of work.

2. I feel a sense of purpose and enjoyment from activities outside of my career.

3. I make time for leisure activities that help me relax and de-stress.

4. I feel a sense of balance between my work responsibilities and leisure pursuits.

5. I am able to disconnect from work and truly enjoy my free time.

Now, add up your points and use the scale below as a measuring tool.

Total Points	Results
80 - 100	Overall, you seem very satisfied with various aspects of your life. Keep nurturing the areas that bring you joy and fulfillment!
60 - 79	You're generally satisfied, but there might be room for improvement in certain areas. Consider which questions scored lower and brainstorm ways to address those aspects.
40 - 59	Your current level of satisfaction might require some adjustments. Talk to a trusted friend, family member, therapist, or healthcare provider about areas you'd like to improve.
Below 40	Consider seeking professional support from a therapist or counselor to explore strategies for enhancing your overall well-being.

After answering all the questions, take a moment to reflect on your answers. Are there any areas that score consistently lower than the rest? This might be an indication that an aspect of your life needs a little more attention. But remember, this is just the starting point. Use this information to identify areas where you might want to make changes and create a plan to reach a higher level of overall satisfaction.

Finding Fulfillment

Finding activities outside of work, and sometimes outside of your family, that spark joy and fulfillment is crucial for a balanced life. But sometimes, amidst daily routines, it's easy to lose touch with what truly ignites our passions. Here are some strategies to help you rediscover the activities that bring you back to life:

- **Memory lane:** Close your eyes and travel back to times when you felt truly fulfilled and engaged. Were you lost in a creative project? Fully immersed in nature? Sharing laughter with friends? Jot down these memories and identify the common threads. What aspects of the experience brought you joy?

- **Childhood passions:** Think back to your childhood hobbies and interests. Did you love building forts? Drawing fantastical creatures? Playing a musical instrument? Reconnecting with these forgotten passions can reignite a spark or inspire new avenues to explore.

- **What matters most:** What are your core values? Do you value creativity, learning, helping others, or spending time in nature? Aligning your hobbies with your values can create a deeper sense of purpose and fulfillment.

- **The routine break:** Don't be afraid to experiment! Trying new activities, from rock climbing to pottery classes, can lead to surprising discoveries. You might find a hidden talent or a newfound passion.

- **The spark within:** Pay attention to how you feel during activities. Do you lose track of time? Feel a surge of energy? Get completely absorbed in the process? These are signs you've stumbled upon something special.

- **Community connection:** Look for opportunities to connect with others who share your interests. Joining a club, taking a class, or participating in online forums can provide camaraderie and support as you delve deeper into your hobbies. One way that I incorporate this principle into my life is by making time to play *Bunco* once a month with all my girlfriends.

Remember, finding fulfilling hobbies is a process of exploration and self-discovery. Don't get discouraged if you don't find your perfect activity right away. Embrace the exploration, have fun, and, most importantly, reconnect with the joy that lies outside of work.

Actions for Improvement

The key to a balanced and fulfilling life is understanding where you are struggling with balance and then taking action to correct it. Here's how to translate the insights from the quiz into concrete steps.

Reignite Your Career Spark

If your career score was low, consider opportunities for growth. Research professional development courses, attend industry workshops, or speak to your supervisor about mentorship programs. Look for ways to personalize your current role. Can you take on new responsibilities that align with your skills and interests? Discuss possibilities for project assignments or adjustments to your daily tasks to create a more fulfilling work experience.

Cultivate Meaningful Connections

Schedule regular quality time with loved ones. Plan activities you all enjoy, have in-depth conversations, and express your appreciation. Build a strong social support network. Reconnect with old friends, join a club, or volunteer for a cause you care about. Having a sense of belonging and connection strengthens overall well-being. These aren't huge time commitments. You may even just meet a friend for your 30-60-minute lunch during the week. Just find time to connect, no matter how long the connection will last.

Create a Balanced Life Blueprint

Set SMART goals (Specific, Measurable, Achievable, Relevant, and Time-bound) that encompass different areas of your life. These could include taking a weekend trip every quarter, joining a gym, or learning a new language. Identify your non-negotiables—the things you absolutely need to make time for—and schedule them first. Learn to politely decline commitments that conflict with your priorities or well-being.

Change takes time and effort. Be patient with yourself, celebrate your progress, and don't be afraid to adjust your approach along the way. By taking these actions, you can create a life that feels balanced, fulfilling, and true to who you are. For this chapter's self-reflection and activity moment, we'll continue exploring what excites us and makes us feel satisfied while creating a visual representation of what our lives currently look like.

Chapter Activity and Reflection Moment

Ever feel like you're spinning too many plates? The Work-Life Balance Wheel is a handy tool to help you see how well you're juggling all the important parts of your life. It's basically a pie chart, but instead of slices of food, you have slices representing different areas, like work, family, health, and hobbies. By coloring in each section based on your satisfaction level, you can easily identify areas that need a little more attention. So, let's each create our own work-life balance wheel and take control of our lives.

Step 1: Identify Your Key Life Domains

Grab a pen and some paper, and get ready to brainstorm! Think about the different areas of your life that contribute to your overall well-being. This might include work, family, relationships, health, leisure, personal development, finances, spirituality, or anything else that's important to you. There's no right or wrong answer here: choose what resonates most with you!

Step 2: Draw Your Wheel

Now, let's create the visual. On your paper, draw a large circle. Divide this circle into sections, like slices of a pie. You can choose to make them all the same size, or you can adjust the size of each section based on how important that area feels in your life. For example, if family is a huge priority, you might give that section a larger slice.

Step 3: Rate Your Satisfaction

Time to get honest! Each section of your wheel represents one of your life domains. Imagine a scale of 1 to 10, with 1 being the least satisfied and 10 being the most satisfied. Consider factors like time spent, energy invested, enjoyment gained, and overall sense of fulfillment. Write a number inside each section of your wheel that reflects your current level of satisfaction for that domain.

Step 4: Color It In!

Here comes the fun part! Grab some colored pencils, crayons, or markers (get creative!). Use different colors or shades to fill in each section of your wheel, corresponding to the satisfaction rating you assigned. A brightly colored section indicates high satisfaction, while a lightly shaded or blank section indicates a lower level of satisfaction.

Step 5: Reflect and Analyze

Take a moment to step back and admire your handiwork! Now comes the powerful part—reflection and analysis. Look at the overall shape of your wheel. Is it a smooth circle, or does it have some lopsided sections? Are there areas that are brightly colored, indicating high satisfaction? What about areas that are barely shaded, suggesting a need for improvement?

Step 6: Set Goals for Improvement

Based on your observations, it's time to take action! Identify areas where your wheel needs a boost. Set SMART goals (Specific, Measurable, Achievable, Relevant, and Time-Bound) to address these imbalances. Let's use the example of wanting to improve your sleep quality so that you have more energy during the day. Here's what your SMART goal might look like:

- **Specific:** I will establish a consistent sleep schedule, aiming for 7-8 hours of sleep each night.

- **Measurable:** For the next four weeks, I will track my sleep duration and quality using a sleep-tracking app.

- **Attainable:** Instead of drastically changing my bedtime right away, I will set a goal to adjust my sleep schedule by 15 minutes earlier each week.

- **Relevant:** Better sleep will increase my focus and energy, allowing me to be more productive at work and have more fulfilling personal interactions.

- **Time-Bound:** I will commit to following this sleep schedule for four weeks, then re-evaluate my progress and adjust the goal if needed.

By following these SMART principles, I can increase my chances of achieving this sleep goal and reaping the benefits of better-quality sleep.

Step 7: Review and Refine

Your Work-Life Balance Wheel isn't a one-time snapshot. Life is dynamic, and your priorities may shift. Revisit your wheel periodically, maybe every few months or a year. Update your ratings and shading based on your current situation. As you achieve goals and make adjustments, you'll see your wheel evolve, reflecting a more balanced and fulfilling life.

Once you've created your wheel, remember that this isn't the end. If it's way out of balance, see it as encouragement to continue on this journey. In the next chapter, we'll explore strategies for achieving work-life balance based on all the insight we've gained so far, so buckle up! We're just getting started!

Chapter 3:

Strategies for Achieving Work-Life Balance

Don't get so busy making a living that you forget to make a life. –Dolly Parton

Have you ever noticed someone washing dishes angrily? You know, when the mugs are shoved under the water with the same intention as waterboarding someone? Or when you hear the cutlery being thrown into the water passive-aggressively? Well, guilty as charged yet again! That's right, I used to be an aggressive dishwasher. Why? Because I did it from a place of resentment. While my kids were already fast asleep in their warm bed and my husband was speedily on his way to dreamland, I would stand in the cold, lonely kitchen, washing dishes. Why? Because a good wife and mother never goes to bed with a dirty kitchen! Or do they?

Honestly, I'm not sure what the root of that particular belief of mine was, but for a very long time, I believed it like I believe in gravity. I thought my children and my husband would be embarrassed by me if I ever left the dishes for the following day. So, I would do them at midnight, right after ensuring that every other spot in the house was also spotless. I thought it was expected and that my husband would call his mother in horror the moment I stopped doing it. So, instead, I turned into a drama queen, armed with a sponge and dish soap. Until one day, a friend said something that changed my entire worldview. She said, "When someone doesn't do something, it's because it's not important to them." I contemplated her wisdom and then turned it on its head: What you do with your time shows what is important to you.

The message I had been sending to my family all those times was loud and clear: A clean kitchen is more important than a bedtime story. Or, a clean kitchen is more important than going to bed with my husband. They weren't in the kitchen scrubbing the pots until midnight because, you guessed it, they literally didn't care! My husband didn't expect me to always have a clean kitchen, and he didn't judge me for not double-rinsing the new Tupperware. I realized that I had this unrealistic expectation—and only of myself. My friends' dirty kitchens didn't bother me one bit, so why was I so obsessed with mine? From that day forward, I decided to let my time speak for itself as to what I find important. Now, I spend time cuddling with my kids, watching a movie after dinner, or actually getting more than six hours of sleep. I prioritize myself over the expectations I used to have.

In this chapter, we'll continue to explore this idea of time management. We'll look at strategies to align your core values along with how you spend your time. We'll also explore the role healthy boundaries can play when it comes to time management and how to manage stress and prevent burnout. Are you excited to put that deathly sponge down and find your peace even when your kitchen is dirty? Let's jump straight in, then!

Aligning Actions With Happiness and Expectations

Take a quick look at your schedule. Chances are, your daily life is a juggling act between these three types of tasks: the genuinely happy, the obligatory, and the expectation-driven. Here's a breakdown to help you tell them apart and why it's important to understand the difference.

Genuine Happiness Tasks

These tasks are the stars of the show! These are activities you do purely for the enjoyment they bring. Imagine getting lost in a good book, mastering a new song on guitar, or sharing laughter with close friends. These tasks are intrinsically motivated, meaning you do them for the sheer pleasure and fulfillment they provide. They energize you and leave you feeling accomplished, tapping into your core interests and values.

Obligatory Tasks

On the other hand, obligatory tasks are the unsung heroes. They might not be inherently exciting, but they contribute to the smooth running of your life. Think of things like paying bills, grocery shopping, or cleaning the house. These tasks are extrinsically motivated, meaning you do them because they need to be done, even if they don't spark immediate joy. While not inherently pleasurable, they shouldn't be soul-crushing, either. The key to obligatory tasks is to find ways to make them efficient, perhaps using tools or delegating, when possible, to free up more time for the happy stuff. Something that helped me tremendously in this area is making use of online grocery shopping, where they deliver it to your door, or you can simply stop and pick it up on your way home.

Expectation-Driven Tasks

These tasks walk a tightrope between obligation and social pressure. Some activities you do because you feel you "should," not necessarily because you want to. Imagine staying late at work to impress your boss, even if the extra hours don't genuinely interest you, or attending a social event you don't enjoy because you feel obligated. Expectation-driven tasks can be a source of inauthenticity and stress. They are often linked to societal or professional pressures that may not align with your true values or interests. While some social expectations can't be entirely avoided, it's important to be mindful of them and challenge those that don't truly serve you.

These different types of tasks fill our daily lives. Whether we plan it or not, at the end of the day, you would've completed activities from these lists. However, by planning our schedules, we get to choose how much time and energy we want to devote to each group. To do so, we need to know what we value in life to ensure that our core values align with our daily actions as well. Otherwise, our tasks will only reflect expectations and obligations. To achieve true joy and happiness, we need to align our actions with the tasks that bring us joy and fulfillment. Let's take a minute to identify our core values.

Identifying Core Values

Core values are the fundamental principles that guide your life choices and overall well-being (Sutler-Cohen, 2019). They represent what truly matters to you and impact how you interact with the world and make decisions. Identifying your core values is crucial for achieving a healthy work-life balance for a few key reasons, such as providing you with clarity and direction, encouraging boundaries, and keeping you motivated and fulfilled. By taking the time to identify your core values, you gain a deeper understanding of yourself and what brings you true satisfaction (Sutler-Cohen, 2019). This empowers you to make intentional choices that create a healthy work-life balance and a life filled with purpose. So, with that in mind, here are a few exercises that you can use to identify your core values:

- **Life role model analysis:** Think about people you admire (historical figures, fictional characters, or people you know). What qualities do you respect most in them (e.g., honesty, courage, creativity)? Why do these qualities resonate with you?

- **Ideal future vision:** Imagine your ideal future self—what kind of life are you living? What are your accomplishments, and how did you achieve them? What principles guided your decisions and actions?

- **Deal-breakers:** Consider situations in which you felt strongly opposed to something. What values were being violated in those scenarios (e.g., fairness, integrity)?

Now, based on the answers to these exercises, brainstorm a list of core values that resonate with you. Don't worry about quantity; focus on what feels authentic. Review your list and narrow it down to 3-5 core values that are most important to you currently. This will be your guiding compass. Then, consider the tasks you spend most of your time on. Do they align with these core values of yours? If not, how can you adjust your choices of tasks tomorrow? By consistently reflecting and making conscious choices, you can bridge the gap between your values and daily actions. This will lead to a more fulfilling life where your purpose is clear, and your actions reflect your deepest convictions.

Strategies for Prioritizing Activities

Hypothetically speaking, you've now established your core values, and you can choose to prioritize activities that are within your values, but it sounds a little too good to be true, right? Well, that's because all of this is based on the idea that we get to choose what we prioritize. The problem comes in when we don't know how to prioritize or what it even means. Prioritizing can be harder than we might think. Prioritizing refers to the process of organizing tasks or activities based on their importance and urgency. It's essentially deciding which things need to be done first and why. It empowers you to take control of your time and energy, and it allows you to be more productive, achieve your goals, and, ultimately, live a less stressful and more fulfilling life. But *how*? How do we practically prioritize? Here are a few strategies that you can rely on to help with prioritizing.

The Eisenhower Matrix

The Eisenhower Matrix is a popular tool for prioritizing tasks based on their urgency and importance. It helps you visualize your to-do list and decide which tasks to tackle first, delegate, or even eliminate altogether. Here's a breakdown of how it works (*The Eisenhower Matrix*, 2022).

The Grid

Imagine a square divided into four quadrants by a horizontal and vertical line. The horizontal line represents urgency (urgent vs. not urgent), and the vertical line represents importance (important vs. not important). This creates four distinct areas:

- **Urgent and important (do first):** These are tasks that demand your immediate attention and have a significant impact on your goals or well-being. Examples include meeting deadlines, responding to emergencies, or addressing critical issues.

- **Not urgent and important (schedule):** These are tasks that contribute to your long-term goals but aren't time-sensitive. Examples include planning projects, exercising, or engaging in self-development activities. Schedule dedicated time for these in your calendar.

- **Urgent and not important (delegate):** These are often time-sensitive but don't necessarily contribute to your goals. Examples include answering unimportant emails, responding to interruptions, or handling low-priority errands. Consider delegating them to free up your time for more important tasks.

- **Not urgent and not important (eliminate):** These are tasks that neither require immediate attention nor contribute significantly to your goals. Examples include excessive social media scrolling, unproductive meetings, or time-wasting activities. Eliminate them whenever possible.

Using the Matrix

1. **List your tasks:** Write down all the tasks you need to accomplish, both work-related and personal.

2. **Categorize each task:** Analyze each task based on urgency and importance. Is it time-sensitive and critical (urgent)? Does it contribute to your long-term goals (important)? Place each task in the appropriate quadrant of the matrix.

3. **Take action:** Once categorized, prioritize your actions. Focus on tackling tasks in the "Do First" quadrant first. Schedule time

for important but not urgent tasks. Delegate or eliminate tasks in the remaining quadrants.

The Eisenhower Matrix is a simple yet powerful tool that can help you gain control of your to-do list and prioritize activities that contribute to your overall well-being and goals (*The Eisenhower Matrix*, 2022).

The Value vs. Complexity Matrix

The Value vs. Complexity Matrix is a prioritization tool that helps you decide which tasks to tackle first based on their potential benefit (value) and the effort (complexity) required to complete them (Uniyal, 2023). It allows you to visualize your tasks and determine the optimal balance between maximizing value and managing the resources needed to achieve it. It is similar to The Eisenhower Matrix, but it focuses more on benefit and effort rather than importance and urgency.

The Grid

Again, imagine a square divided into four quadrants by a horizontal and vertical line. The horizontal line represents the complexity of the task (low vs. high complexity), and the vertical line represents the value it delivers (high vs. low value).

This creates four distinct areas:

- **High value, low complexity (quick wins):** These are ideal tasks to tackle first. They offer significant benefits (high value) with minimal effort or time investment (low complexity). Completing these tasks provides a quick boost to your progress and motivates further action.

- **High value, high complexity (big bets):** These tasks hold the potential for significant rewards (high value) but require substantial planning, resources, or effort (high complexity) to complete. They might be strategic projects or initiatives with long-term benefits. Carefully evaluate these tasks before diving in, and consider breaking them down into smaller, more manageable steps.

- **Low value, low complexity (trivial tasks):** These tasks require minimal effort (low complexity) but offer little benefit (low value). While they might be easy to complete, they don't significantly contribute to your goals. Consider delegating or eliminating them whenever possible to free up time and energy for more impactful activities.

- **Low value, high complexity (time sucks):** These tasks are resource-heavy (high complexity) but offer minimal return (low value). They are often time-consuming and drain your energy without delivering significant results. Avoid these tasks whenever possible or find ways to streamline or eliminate them altogether.

Using the Matrix

1. **List your tasks:** Write down all the tasks you need to accomplish.

2. **Complete a value and complexity assessment:** For each task, determine its relative value (high vs. low) and complexity (high vs. low). Consider the potential impact of the task on your goals (value) and the time, resources, and effort required to complete it (complexity).

3. **Plot the tasks:** Place each task in the appropriate quadrant of the matrix based on your assessment.

4. **Prioritize actions:** Focus on tackling tasks in the "Quick Wins" quadrant first. These provide a high return on investment for your time and effort. High Value, High Complexity tasks might require further planning or breaking down into smaller steps before beginning. Low-value tasks can be delegated or eliminated to free up time for more impactful activities.

This method is particularly useful for product managers, project managers, or anyone who needs to prioritize tasks based on their long-term strategic value and the resources available (which includes all parents, regardless of your occupation).

The Pomodoro Method

The Pomodoro Technique is a time management system that breaks down work into focused intervals, promoting increased productivity and preventing burnout. It's a simple yet highly effective method for better time management, and it helps prioritize the things in your life on which you want to focus more. Here's how you can use it (Sheldon & Wigmore, 2022).

The Process

1. **Choose a task:** Select a single, important task you want to complete.

2. **Set the timer:** Use a timer (traditionally a tomato-shaped timer, hence the name "Pomodoro," which is Italian for tomato) for 25 minutes.

3. **Work with focus:** Eliminate distractions and concentrate solely on the chosen task until the timer rings.

4. **Short break:** Take a short, five-minute break to refresh your mind. Get up, move around, grab a drink, or do some stretches.

5. **Repeat:** Return to steps 1-4 for three more Pomodoros (25 minutes of work followed by a 5-minute break).

6. **Long break:** After completing four Pomodoros, take a longer break of 15-30 minutes.

If you don't want to make use of this particular process, there are also many Pomodoro apps available online and on mobile devices. You can also adjust your timer if 25 minutes feels too short. Experiment with longer intervals until you find what works best for you. The most important aspect is to avoid checking emails, social media, or other distractions during the work interval. These are often the time-wasters that steal most of our precious time allocated to something else. By following these steps and incorporating the Pomodoro Technique into your routine, you can experience increased productivity, reduced stress, and a better work-life balance.

These three techniques are great starting blocks for learning to prioritize the important things in your life. However, they also teach you another essential tool: time management!

Mastering Time Management

Time management is the process of planning and controlling how you spend your time. It's about consciously organizing your activities to achieve your goals in the most efficient and effective way. There are four key components to time management:

- **Planning:** This involves setting goals, identifying tasks, and creating a schedule for completing them. It's about deciding what needs to be done and when.

- **Prioritization:** Not all tasks are created equal. Effective time management involves determining which tasks are most important and allocating your time accordingly.

- **Organization**: This includes techniques like creating to-do lists, setting deadlines, and utilizing calendars to keep track of your commitments.

- **Focus and efficiency:** Time management is about minimizing distractions and maximizing your productivity while working on a task. It involves avoiding procrastination and utilizing strategies to stay focused and complete tasks in a timely manner.

Time management is essential, as you probably know by now. I remember a time in my life when I tried my best to do everything for everyone while also establishing boundaries and taking care of myself. I had a whole schedule planned with a list of self-care activities to enjoy after work. Yet, it never happened! After work, I would fall down on the couch or make dinner and clean. One day, I phoned a good friend of mine and told her that I simply didn't have time to exercise or to take care of myself. She listened as I spoke and gently pointed out to me that the problem wasn't not having enough time. The problem was my time management.

I learned from that experience the importance of showing yourself some grace and being okay with not getting some things done. Your to-do list is always there with a few items that inherently stay on the list. Over time, you decide they aren't that important, and they eventually drop off. If you use the techniques described above, these things may not ever make the list to begin with. So, if you're in the shoes I was in, convinced that you have fewer hours in a day than most other people do, then buckle up! It's time to learn how to master time management, starting with how to prioritize and delegate.

Prioritize and Delegate

Do you remember when you created a list of your core values? Keep these core values in mind as you enter this section and begin to prioritize your tasks. Prioritizing refers to the art of arranging your tasks based on their significance and urgency. It's about deciding what matters most and tackling those things first. Imagine your to-do list as a battlefield. Prioritization involves identifying the critical objectives, the ones that will have the biggest impact on your goals. These are the high-ground positions you need to secure first. Less critical tasks, while still requiring attention, can be addressed later or even eliminated if necessary. By prioritizing effectively, you ensure you're focusing your energy on the activities that truly move the needle forward and the things that matter.

Delegation, on the other hand, is the act of entrusting specific tasks or responsibilities to others. It's not about dumping work; it's about recognizing that some activities can be completed just as well, or even better, by someone else. Imagine you're leading a military campaign. You, as the general, have a strategic vision and a vast battlefield to manage. Delegating tasks to skilled lieutenants allows you to focus on the bigger picture while ensuring all aspects of the operation are addressed effectively. Delegation empowers others to use their skills and frees you up to tackle the high-level tasks that require your unique expertise. When done correctly, delegation becomes a force multiplier, allowing you to achieve more than you ever could alone. Both prioritizing and delegating are crucial for maximizing your effectiveness and achieving a healthy work-life balance.

If you're like me, though, the thought of delegating might send a cold shiver down your spine. Learning how to delegate is probably one of the hardest things I ever had to learn. Why? Because my inner control freak convinces me time and time again that I am the only one capable of doing something, even when I know that it's not the case. I'm so terrified of dumping work on others that I would rather just do it myself and know that it's done correctly. But you know where that mindset got me? Very near to burnout. We simply can't do everything on our own; it's not humanly possible. But not all tasks are "delegate-friendly." Let's take a look at how to know which tasks to delegate.

When to Delegate

Determining which tasks to delegate involves analyzing the task itself and your own capabilities. First, you need to consider the skill and expertise required. Ask yourself these two questions.

- Does the task require your unique skills and knowledge? Certain tasks demand your specific expertise or experience to be completed effectively. These are likely not good candidates for delegation.

- Can someone else on your team complete the task with the necessary skills and experience? Look for opportunities to delegate tasks that align with someone else's strengths and areas of expertise. This leverages their skills and allows them to develop further.

- What about at home? Are you the only person who cooks dinner? Could you delegate a couple of nights to others each week to free time up to do other things or take better care of yourself? I recently asked my family to take two to three nights of planning/cooking each week to allow me time to write, work out, and do things I love to do. They happily said yes, and we have incorporated this change into our weeks. This one thing has freed up a couple of hours per week, and it feels fantastic!

Next, consider the urgency and the importance of the task you're considering to delegate:

- Is the task urgent or critical? If a task demands immediate attention and has a significant impact on your goals, it might be best for you to handle it yourself.

- Is delegating the task likely to cause delays or affect the quality of the outcome? Urgent and critical tasks might require your direct oversight.

Once you've answered those questions, you might have a clearer picture of whether this task is delegate-friendly. Next, consider the task's time constraints:

- Do you have the time to complete the task yourself, considering your workload and priorities? If you're swamped with high-priority tasks, delegating less critical items can free up your time to focus on what matters most.

- Could someone else complete the task more efficiently, given their current workload? Consider the overall time investment required. Delegation might be beneficial if someone else can complete it quickly.

Finally, consider the learning and the development of the task:

- Is the task repetitive or routine? Delegating such tasks allows you to focus on more strategic work.

- Could someone else benefit from the learning experience of completing this task? Delegation can be a valuable opportunity for skill development and empowering others.

By carefully considering these factors, you can identify tasks that are well-suited for delegation. This frees up your time and allows you to focus on your core competencies while empowering others to grow and contribute. Remember, effective delegation is a win-win situation for everyone involved. Now, delegation goes hand in hand with establishing healthy boundaries, so let's move on to understanding boundaries better.

Establishing Healthy Boundaries

Boundaries are invisible lines we draw to define the space between our work lives and personal lives. They establish what is acceptable and unacceptable in terms of our time, energy, and emotional availability. Strong boundaries are crucial for maintaining a healthy work-life balance and overall well-being. Strong boundaries act as a shield, protecting our time, energy, and emotional well-being. By establishing clear boundaries, we can avoid overcommitment. Saying no to extra tasks or setting firm deadlines for existing ones safeguards our personal time and prevents burnout.

These boundaries also minimize distractions, allowing us to be fully present and engaged at work, maximizing productivity. The same applies to our personal lives—clear boundaries ensure we can truly unwind and recharge during leisure time. Furthermore, boundaries foster healthy relationships with colleagues. When expectations are clear, we avoid feeling pressured to be constantly available and establish realistic communication boundaries outside of work hours, leading to mutual respect and understanding. But setting boundaries can be difficult, especially when you're scared of losing out on something. For example, when you say no to working overtime, so you're scared they might not consider you for the next promotion. But boundaries, whether personal or professional, are essential for a healthy work-life balance. Let's take a look at how to establish personal boundaries.

Work Boundaries

Establishing clear boundaries at work protects your time and energy, fostering a healthier work-life balance. You can start building boundaries at work by initiating a conversation with your manager or your employer about your preferred work hours and communication methods. Express your comfort level with tasks such as checking emails and responding to messages outside of designated work hours. You should also be upfront about your workload and propose realistic deadlines for projects. I know it can be intimidating, but don't shy away from pushing back on unrealistic expectations.

Furthermore, if you are often asked to stay late after work, set boundaries by creating a ritual to signify the end of your workday. This could involve shutting down your computer, tidying your workspace, or taking a short walk to signal the shift from work mode to personal time. This is also a great place to utilize technology to your advantage by setting up "Out of Office" emails or switching your work phone to "Do Not Disturb." By combining clear communication, proactive time management, and technological tools, you can effectively establish boundaries at work, reducing stress and promoting a more balanced, fulfilling life. It's important that you don't go back on boundaries that you've created since that will encourage others to push your boundaries on a regular basis.

I recently spoke to a young woman who, at the age of 27, was appointed senior manager at her accounting firm. She was phenomenal at her job and always went above and beyond. Over time, her workload began to increase more and more. More clients were assigned to her division, even though she had the fewest team members, and pretty soon, she had to take over clients from her director. On average, she worked late at least four nights of the week and often used her weekends to catch up on work that her team couldn't finish during the week. Eventually, it got to the point where she had to speak out about it. To her surprise, her employers told her that they didn't understand why it was suddenly a problem since she had been working this late and hard since she started working there. They were shocked by her sudden boundaries since they weren't used to them. She realized that she had to be strict with her boundaries so that they would recognize how overloaded her team was and create a new expectation of her work hours.

It's essential to realize that when you set work boundaries, you may be working at a company where what you value does not align with the culture or values of the company. The company may value long hours and expect you to work them without question. You may be unable to leave if that would mean moving to a new house or city in order to find a new job, or you may have to travel more, etc. Understand that you are choosing to stay in this environment, so you need to be happy with your decision and come to terms with the misalignment of values. Otherwise, I would encourage you to start looking for another job and work on your network in order to attract new opportunities.

Family and Personal Relationship Boundaries

Navigating boundaries within family and personal relationships requires open communication and mutual respect. First, have a conversation with family members about your needs and expectations. Explain your desire for designated "me time" to recharge, even if it's just a short period each day. Be clear about your preferred communication styles, as you might need quiet time after work to unwind, so postpone family discussions until later in the evening. Remember, boundaries are a two-way street, so be sure to respect the limitations set by other family members as well.

When possible, delegate tasks and chores to create a more balanced distribution of responsibilities, preventing you from feeling overwhelmed. In your social circle, politely decline invitations when you're feeling drained. A simple "Thank you, but I have other plans tonight" is perfectly acceptable. If attending a social event, decide beforehand how long you'll stay and stick to that timeframe. You can also manage social media to create boundaries. Consider taking breaks from these platforms or muting notifications to avoid the pressure of being constantly connected. Finally, if you find yourself in an uncomfortable situation with a friend or acquaintance, directly but politely communicate your boundaries. Remember, you deserve to feel respected and comfortable in your interactions with others.

It's totally okay not to want to have your in-laws over for dinner every week. Don't relent on your boundaries because you're scared of hurting other people's feelings. By openly communicating and expressing your needs in a kind manner, those who truly care for you will understand. Perhaps this activity will help you to grasp the importance of boundaries.

Chapter Activity and Reflection Moment

Close your eyes and take a few deep breaths. Feel your body settle and your mind begin to quiet. Imagine yourself standing in the center of a vast field. This field represents your life energy, a precious resource you share with the world. Look around. Notice a shimmering fence bordering the field. This fence symbolizes your boundaries, the lines that define what you're willing to share and protect.

Think about your work life. Can colleagues easily reach you outside of work hours? Do you feel pressured to take on extra tasks that drain your energy? Imagine strengthening the section of the fence around your work area. Now, consider your personal life. How much time do you dedicate to yourself and your loved ones? Do you find yourself constantly pulled in different directions? Imagine reinforcing the fence around your personal space, allowing only those who nourish you to enter freely.

Boundaries aren't walls; they're filters. They allow you to give generously while protecting your well-being. Breathe deeply again, feeling the strength of your newly reinforced boundaries. You have the right to protect your energy, both professionally and personally. Open your eyes, carrying this sense of empowered self-care with you throughout your day. Remember, strong boundaries are the foundation for a fulfilling and balanced life.

You can repeat this meditation as often as you need to remind yourself of the importance of boundaries in your life. In the next chapter, we'll discuss the importance of family and friends who care about you as we explore the importance of nurturing healthy relationships.

Chapter 4:

Nurturing Relationships—Give Yourself and Others Grace

The most important thing is to enjoy your life—to be happy—it's all that matters.
—Audrey Hepburn

Have you ever been in a friendship that felt...off? Perhaps you felt like you had to be perfect all the time, or maybe you left every get-together feeling drained and completely exhausted? Well, that might be a sign of a not-so-healthy friendship. Let me assure you that you're not alone. In fact, 84% of women report having been in a toxic friendship (Cline, 2020). That's pretty wild! Unfortunately, once we've experienced relationships and friendships that are slightly toxic, we build walls and disguise them as boundaries. We tell ourselves that if a friend doesn't do this, this, and this, then we'll cut them out of our lives. While it's essential to have boundaries and protect yourself from toxic people, you should be careful that you don't become the toxic one in turn.

Nurturing relationships that are healthy and good for both parties requires grace. It requires understanding that some days, we're just not as chirpy, and on other days, we might show up late to dinner because of a work emergency. But it's important to know that nurturing friendships also takes a lot of energy and won't just maintain itself. But if you want to have it all, you need to have solid people in your life and, therefore, nurture healthy relationships. That's why this chapter is all about understanding the importance of healthy relationships, embracing imperfections, and building supportive relationships. So, are you ready to make *best friends forever* bracelets and build healthy relationships?

The Importance of Healthy Relationships

Even when life throws a whirlwind of commitments our way, investing time and energy in healthy friendships and relationships remains paramount. These connections are essential pillars of our well-being. Strong social bonds provide emotional support, a sense of belonging, and a source of joy. They act as a buffer against stress, helping us navigate life's challenges with greater resilience. Sharing laughter, confiding in trusted friends, and celebrating victories together fosters a sense of connection that enriches our lives. Healthy relationships also encourage personal growth.

Friends and loved ones can challenge us to step outside our comfort zones, offer different perspectives, and inspire us to be better versions of ourselves. While a jam-packed schedule might tempt us to prioritize work or errands over social connections, neglecting these bonds can lead to feelings of isolation, depression, and loneliness (Abrams, 2023). By consciously scheduling time for loved ones and nurturing our friendships, even in small ways, we invest in our happiness and overall well-being, creating a richer and more fulfilling life experience.

I've learned that even when I travel for work, I prioritize the people that I love, as it keeps me grounded and filled with joy. Whenever I travel, I miss my three daughters and my husband terribly, but getting to see friends who live far away or catching up with family I usually only see over the holidays fills me with joy and peace. Keeping in touch with friends, even just for a quick coffee or a drink after work, is a wonderful way to stay connected and never feel too far away from those I love. It's so essential to surround yourself with people who help you become a better person, and I am grateful that I have those kinds of people in my life. If you don't, I have great news: It's not too late! The first step to nurturing healthy relationships and good friendships starts by embracing imperfections.

Embracing Imperfections

No one is perfect; let's just get that straight for a moment. No friendship is perfect, and that's okay. Life isn't about perfection! I once heard someone say that if a friend takes more than three days to respond to your text, you should cut them out of your life. To that, I say, "Where's the grace?" I've been at points in my life where I was so tired I couldn't get out of bed. Or where seasonal depression would cripple me with anxiety, and responding to texts felt impossible. On other occasions, I've simply been so busy with work, prepping for a major project, or hosting the entire family over Christmas that connecting with friends just wasn't possible. And you know what? I am so grateful that none of my friends decided to "cut me out" during those times of silence. The beauty is, neither would I! Friendships, like people, aren't perfect. But that's okay! Let's explore how to appreciate the quirks and flaws that come with the territory.

- **Shift your perspective:** The first step to embracing imperfections starts by recognizing that imperfections make us unique. We all have our little oddities and baggage, and these quirks are often what make our friends interesting and relatable. By shifting our perspective, we also get to focus on the good instead of dwelling on the things that bother us.

- **Practice acceptance:** Next, we need to accept that we can't change people. Trying to mold your friend into someone they're not will only lead to frustration. Accept them for who they are, flaws and all. If something truly bothers you, talk to your friend openly and honestly. But focus on "I" statements and finding solutions together.

- **Celebrate the real:** Finally, to embrace imperfections, we need to celebrate that friendship is a two-way street. Embrace your own flaws and appreciate that your friends accept you for who you are. Having real friends is way more valuable than having friends who try to be perfect all the time.

Friendships are about grace and support and love, not meeting certain expectations in order to appear like the perfect friend. So, embrace those imperfections and choose to love your friends even when they don't answer your texts immediately. By embracing imperfections, you open the door to supporting relationships.

Building Supportive Relationships

Building supportive relationships and friendships takes time and effort, but the rewards are immense. Here's a roadmap to get you started (Mental Health Foundation, 2023):

- **Be a good listener:** Pay genuine attention to what others have to say, show empathy, and avoid interrupting. This builds trust and fosters a safe space for open communication.

- **Show genuine interest:** Be curious and actively ask questions about their lives, hobbies, and passions. People appreciate feeling seen and heard.

- **Be reliable and trustworthy:** Follow through on commitments and keep your word. This builds trust and strengthens the bond.

- **Offer support and encouragement:** Be there for your friends during tough times, but also celebrate their successes.

- **Be open and share yourself:** Let your true self shine through, including your vulnerabilities. This fosters deeper connections and allows others to reciprocate.

- **Be respectful of boundaries:** Everyone needs personal space. Respect your friends' need for time alone, and avoid being clingy.

- **Maintain a positive attitude:** A positive outlook is contagious. Focus on the good and avoid negativity.

- **Be proactive:** Don't wait for others to reach out. Take initiative to plan activities, suggest outings, or simply send a thoughtful message to stay connected.

Remember, friendships are a two-way street. By putting in the effort to cultivate these qualities, you'll attract supportive people who enrich your life and create a network of genuine connections that will see you through life's ups and downs.

Toxic vs. Healthy Relationships

Have you ever looked back on a past relationship or failed friendship and thought to yourself, "How did I not see the signs?" You're not the only one! We all deal with not-so-nice people along the way to finding healthy and solid relationships, but that doesn't mean that we can't be on the lookout for them. We don't want to end up investing all our time and energy into someone who isn't a healthy fit for us, right? That doesn't mean that we expect perfection from everyone in our lives, but it does mean that there are certain things we shouldn't be willing to tolerate. Discerning between healthy and toxic people in your life can be tricky, but it's crucial for establishing strong support systems and prioritizing your well-being. Here's a breakdown of key traits to watch out for in both toxic and healthy people (Casarella, 2022).

Signs of Toxic People

- **Energy drainers:** Do you feel depleted and emotionally exhausted after interacting with toxic people? They often drain your energy with negativity, complaining, or drama. You don't have to stop being friends with them; you just need to moderate your time with them.
- **Disrespectful behavior:** Do they constantly criticize you, put you down, or make fun of you? Healthy relationships are built on mutual respect and kindness.

- **Unreliability and dishonesty:** Can you count on them? Do they break promises or make excuses frequently? Toxicity thrives on unreliability and dishonesty.

- **Negative outlook:** Do they constantly see the dark side of things? Negativity can be contagious, and a toxic person's pessimism can bring you down. My best friend has a fairly negative baseline happiness, even though she would call it *realistic*. I enjoy spending time with her, but I can only hang out in small doses because I feel drained by our misalignment of positive energies. That doesn't mean I should cut her out completely but just be aware of our limitations. I still love her endlessly, and she will always be my best friend.

- **Boundaries violations:** Do they constantly overstep your boundaries, disregard your needs, or pressure you into things you're uncomfortable with? Healthy relationships respect personal boundaries.

- **Takers, not givers:** Are they always the ones needing something but rarely offering support or reciprocating favors? Healthy relationships are a two-way street built on mutual give and take.

Signs of Healthy People

- **Supportive and encouraging:** Do they lift you up, celebrate your successes, and offer a shoulder to cry on during tough times? Healthy relationships provide a steady source of support and encouragement.

- **Positive and uplifting:** Do they bring joy and laughter into your life? Their positive outlook can be contagious and enrich your overall well-being.

- **Respectful and trustworthy:** Can you confide in them without judgment? They respect your boundaries, keep their promises, and are trustworthy confidantes.

- **Good listening skills:** Do they actively listen to you, offer empathy, and make you feel heard and understood? Healthy relationships are built on open communication and genuine interest in others.

- **Emotionally available:** Do they make time for you and show genuine interest in your life? They are emotionally available and invest in nurturing the friendship.

- **Respectful of boundaries:** Do they respect your need for personal space and time alone? Healthy relationships understand and respect boundaries.

By recognizing these signs, you can identify the people who uplift, support, and enrich your life. Prioritize spending time and nurturing relationships with these positive individuals. It's okay to distance yourself from those who consistently bring negativity or disrespect into your life. Remember, surrounding yourself with supportive, healthy relationships is crucial for your well-being and happiness. Let's put all of this amazing information into practice as we explore this chapter activity.

Chapter Activity and Reflection Moment

Let's face it: Life gets busy! No matter how much I want to spend every weekend with my friends, talking about life and catching up, it doesn't always work that way. But I've learned over the years to not just *wait* until we can all catch up again but actively plan and schedule my time with friends. I know it doesn't sound as exciting as in the movies where the friends just show up or see each other every single day, but it's probably a way more accurate and effective way to approach cultivating healthy friendships. One of the things my friends and I do each year is Mother's Day Pedicures. We meet for pedicures at 2 p.m. on a set date, get martinis at a local restaurant, and then meet our husbands out for dinner. We look forward to catching up, and the guys even get to participate!

This activity will help you prioritize scheduling time for the loved ones who matter most.

Step 1: *Reflect on Your Inner Circle*

Grab a pen and paper, or use your digital note app if that's more your style, and think about all the people in your life who bring you joy and support and make you feel loved. These could be family members, close friends, significant others, or even a cherished neighbor. Write down the five most important people within that circle with whom you would like to spend more time.

Step 2: *Schedule Like You Mean It!*

Now that you've got the names, pick an activity you could do with each of the people on your list in the next month. This could be anything from grabbing coffee, going for a walk, attending a local event, or simply having a phone or video call for a heart-to-heart chat. Open your calendar and schedule this activity with a specific date and time. Treat it like an important appointment, and try your best not to cancel or reschedule.

Step 3: *Deepen The Connection*

Now, think beyond the activity. Brainstorm additional ways to connect with each person on your list outside of your scheduled activity. This could be a thoughtful text message, a funny meme you know they'd appreciate, or an offering to help them with a small errand. Perhaps there's someone on your list whom you haven't seen in a while, so why not give them a call and catch up before scheduling a date with them?

Step 4: *Watch the Friendship Bloom*

Once all of that is done, reflect on your circle. Are there any additional people you'd like to get to know better and potentially develop deeper friendships with? Write down the names of one to two people who come to mind. Think of an activity you could propose to get to know them better. This could be grabbing lunch together, inviting them to join you for a coffee date, or attending a local event you both might be interested in.

Remember, consistency is key! By taking these steps and scheduling regular time for connection, you'll nurture and deepen the important relationships in your life. In the next chapter, we'll talk about flexibility, adaptability, and the power of embracing change. So, before you *change* your mind about this book, let's continue! (Yes, that was a shameless pun, and no, it probably won't be the last one in the book).

Chapter 5:

Flexibility and Adaptability—

Embracing Change

The bad news is time flies. The good news is you're the pilot. –Michael Altshuler

When I was younger, I was absolutely rigid in my life. Everything had a way of being done, and I knew exactly what that way was. Everything had to be perfect all the time, and if it wasn't, I felt like a failure. I also had very strict deadlines for myself, especially in my personal life. If something could be planned, I planned it way ahead of time. The thing is, I ended up feeling like a failure because I couldn't live up to the deadlines that I created for myself. I placed these impossible expectations on myself and then went into complete despair when I didn't measure up. Let me share an example.

Christmas cards used to be my *thing*. I thrived on coming up with cute ideas, doing elaborate photoshoots, and sending long updates about everyone with the cards to other family members and friends. One year, as I planned the perfect Christmas card idea, I noticed a disinterest from the family. Of course, I got upset! How could they not want to be part of this incredible idea I planned so meticulously? Well, the disinterest and my offense quickly turned into a family fight, and my husband suggested that we didn't send Christmas cards at all that year. So, I stopped. But when Christmas rolled around, I began receiving messages from other family members. "Where are the cards?" or, "We're so excited to see what you get up to this year!" Again, I felt like a failure.

I realized that by being so rigid with the planning, I forgot what it was all about. Instead of creating a fun moment, getting everyone involved, and updating families we couldn't see often in our lives, I made it another *deadline* that had to be perfect. The solution wasn't stopping but rather shifting my perspective and remembering what truly matters. Now, we send cards every year, but we often take the photos months earlier, like when we're on holiday or when we're celebrating something else. Instead of creating the *best* Christmas card, we now focus on creating a moment that is fun and connecting with family. I also don't have a deadline anymore, as I sometimes send the cards before Thanksgiving and other times only after Christmas. That's the power of being flexible and adaptable, two very important tools if you want to have it all!

Understanding Change

Our lives are an ever-flowing river, constantly encountering bends and unexpected currents. This constant change, while sometimes daunting, is woven into the very fabric of life. It stems from our own growth, the dynamism of our relationships, and the unpredictable nature of the world around us. As we learn and mature, our goals and priorities shift, prompting us to explore new avenues. Our families transform through births, marriages, and even disagreements, requiring us to adapt to new dynamics. Beyond our personal sphere, external events like economic shifts or technological advancements reshape the landscape we navigate. While change can be unsettling, fearing it keeps us stagnant. Instead, embracing change allows us to learn, grow, and discover new possibilities. It's through navigating these shifts that we build resilience and carve unique paths for ourselves (Davachi, 2023). So, the next time change knocks on your door, view it not as a threat but as an invitation to a new adventure. Let's start preparing for the adventure that change might have for us by exploring some of the common changes we might encounter.

Common Changes

Change and uncertainty are inevitable parts of life, and they can come from a variety of sources (Davachi, 2023). The type of change I experience might be completely different than the change you're exposed to, but that doesn't mean that the approach should be any different. However, by understanding where change comes from, we'll be able to adapt and be open to these changes before they happen. By being flexible, we'll be able to flourish within the change. Let's take a look at some of the common changes we encounter.

The first common change we encounter can be found in career transitions. The working world is constantly evolving. New technologies emerge, industries restructure, and job markets shift. This can lead to career changes, either planned (like going back to school for a new degree) or unplanned (like a layoff). These transitions can be exciting opportunities for growth, but they also bring uncertainty about the future. However, they don't have to tip the boat completely if we know how to manage the changes in our lives.

The second change that might happen in your life is family dynamics. Families go through many changes throughout life. Milestones like marriages, births, and deaths can all significantly impact family dynamics. When you have children, having a strong support system is critical to being successful personally and professionally. I often felt that the schools required either my husband or myself to miss work for school days off, for conferences, or, as the kids got older, for sporting events. Having a flexible work schedule became very important. Every time I had to leave work, I felt incredibly guilty, so I would shift my hours around to ensure that I still worked a full day. The only way to address this was to be transparent with my boss as I expressed my needs, and you can do the same thing! You can't assume that your boss won't be open to change unless you ask.

Currently, I have a daughter who cannot drive herself to school yet. I am treasuring this time with her every day as she will start driving in the fall, and these moments will be gone. Luckily, my boss understands this, and I'm so grateful for the time I get to spend with her on the drive to school each day. Additionally, everyday challenges like overcoming illnesses, navigating disagreements, and caring for elderly parents can create uncertainty about the future and require adjustments, like potentially moving to where your parents are located. Another change we have to prepare for is external events. The world around us is full of unpredictable events. These can be local (like a natural disaster or a crime wave in your neighborhood) or global (like economic downturns, pandemics, or political unrest). These events can have a major impact on our lives, forcing us to adapt to new circumstances.

Finally, the fourth and probably the most common change we should expect in our lives is personal growth. As we learn and grow as individuals, our values, priorities, and goals change. This personal evolution can lead us to make changes in our lives, such as pursuing new hobbies, ending relationships, or relocating. While positive, such changes can also create uncertainty as we navigate unfamiliar territory.

Strategies for Embracing Change

Embracing change isn't easy, even when you "enjoy" change in general. While change holds the potential for growth and exciting new beginnings, it's natural to resist it. Our brains crave familiarity and comfort in routine. Take breakfast as an example. Do you eat the same thing every morning? Most people do! Is it because they don't like the taste of any other breakfast? Of course not (at least not for the majority), but because it's a habit and part of their morning routine and ritual to get the day started (Cadario & Morewedge, 2022). Now imagine your breakfast suddenly changing. Would it throw you off when it's just a normal workday? Probably, yes. It's the same with most other changes in our lives as well.

Disrupting that pattern with change can be unsettling, triggering feelings of fear and uncertainty. This is why strategies for embracing change are crucial. By reframing our perspective, taking small steps, and seeking support, we can navigate the discomfort of change and unlock its potential for a more fulfilling life. Let's look at three strategies we can rely on for embracing change.

Cultivate Curiosity and a Growth Mindset

Change often feels like a threat to the stable ground we've built. Instead of fearing the unknown, view it as an exciting opportunity to learn and grow. Approach new situations with curiosity, asking questions and actively seeking out knowledge. Embrace a "growth mindset," believing that your abilities can develop and expand through challenges. This shift in perspective will make change feel less like a hurdle and more like an adventure.

Practice Self-Care and Build Resilience

Change can be stressful, so prioritizing self-care is essential. Make sure you're getting enough sleep, eating healthy foods, and engaging in activities that bring you joy and relaxation. This will help you manage stress levels and build resilience, the ability to bounce back from challenges. A strong foundation of self-care allows you to face change with a sense of calm and confidence.

Find Your Anchors and Celebrate Small Wins

Change can feel disorienting, so it's important to hold on to the things that bring you stability. This could be spending time with loved ones, pursuing a cherished hobby, or maintaining a regular meditation practice. These anchors will provide a sense of grounding amidst the transition. Additionally, celebrate every milestone, no matter how small. Acknowledging your progress, even during small steps, helps maintain motivation and keeps you moving forward through change.

The Importance of Flexibility

Unlocking your full potential hinges on embracing life's inevitable changes, and flexibility is the key that unlocks the door. Change, while sometimes disruptive, can propel you towards growth and experiences you never anticipated. A flexible mindset allows you to adapt to new circumstances, learn new skills, and explore uncharted territories. Instead of clinging to rigid plans, you can bend with the winds of change, finding new and creative solutions to navigate challenges.

Ultimately, flexibility empowers you to seize opportunities that might otherwise pass you by, ultimately leading you down a path that unlocks your true potential and allows you to blossom in ways you never imagined. Embrace the flow of change and watch yourself grow and thrive. Here are three tips for becoming more flexible.

Practice Saying Yes (And No)

While being open to new experiences is important, so is discernment. Don't be afraid to step outside your comfort zone and say "yes" to opportunities that pique your interest, even if they seem unfamiliar. This could be trying a new restaurant type, joining a club you've never considered, or taking on a new project at work. Know your limits and don't be afraid to say "no" to situations that drain your energy or violate your values. Flexibility is about finding a balance between embracing new experiences and protecting your well-being.

Develop Multiple Solutions

Life rarely unfolds exactly as planned. When faced with a challenge, resist the urge to cling to a single solution. Instead, brainstorm multiple approaches. Think outside the box and consider unconventional methods. This mental exercise expands your perspective and increases the chances of finding a solution that works, even in unexpected situations.

Embrace Imperfection and Learn to Let Go

Sometimes, things don't go according to plan, and that's okay. Holding onto rigid expectations or clinging to the past hinders your ability to adapt. Learn to embrace imperfection and accept that some things are simply out of your control. Instead of dwelling on what could have been, focus your energy on what you can control and move forward with a sense of acceptance. By letting go of the need for things to be perfect, you open yourself up to the possibilities that change can bring.

Keep your energy focused on the positive and don't dwell on the negative.

With flexibility and openness to change, you will begin to unlock new strategies to face the changes in your life and unlock deeper creativity.

Cultivating Adaptive Strategies

Creativity and innovation are the dynamic duo of problem-solving, propelling us past obstacles in both work and life. By cultivating creative problem solutions and adaptive strategies, you gain a fresh perspective on the changes in your life. Traditional methods may not always work for novel challenges. Creativity allows us to think outside the box, generate unique solutions, and see problems from new angles. This can lead to breakthroughs and advancements that might have been missed otherwise. Take the cell phone, for example. Someone had to go, "Hey, it's a problem that I can't carry my landline with me. What if it didn't have to be stagnant?" and then solved it so creatively! Imagine what your creative adaptive strategies can lead to.

Creative problem-solving doesn't have to be about reinventing the wheel. It can also involve finding more efficient or effective ways to do things, like getting a dishwasher instead of having arguments about the dirty kitchen. By using creative thinking, we can streamline processes, optimize resource allocation, and ultimately achieve better results. So, how can you cultivate these skills in your own life? Here are some tips to consider:

- **Embrace curiosity:** Question the status quo. Ask "why" and "how" about the world around you. Engage in activities that spark your curiosity, like reading often, exploring new hobbies, or taking classes outside your usual domain.

- **Challenge assumptions:** Don't accept things at face value. Look for underlying reasons and explore alternative interpretations. This will help you break free from mental blocks and approach problems with a fresh perspective.

- **Brainstorm regularly:** Make brainstorming a habit, both individually and collaboratively. Set aside time to generate ideas without judgment. The more ideas you explore, the more likely you are to stumble upon a hidden gem.

- **Experiment and learn from mistakes:** Don't be afraid to experiment and try new things. Even failures hold valuable lessons. Embrace a growth mindset, viewing mistakes as opportunities to learn and improve your creative problem-solving skills. A healthy way to consider a "failure" is to think of it as a time to check and adjust your plan—nothing more or less.

- **Seek inspiration:** Surround yourself with creative people and expose yourself to diverse ideas. Visit museums, attend talks, or read biographies of innovators. The more inspiration you gather, the richer your own creative well becomes.

By incorporating these tips and fostering a culture of creativity and innovation, you'll be well-equipped to tackle any obstacle life throws your way. Remember, the most successful problem solvers aren't afraid to think differently and embrace the power of creative solutions. To practice what we've learned, take your time as you journey through this chapter activity and try a meditation created specifically to embrace change in your life.

Chapter Activity and Reflection Moment

As we know by now, change is inevitable. This meditation is a tool for facing change with grace and flexibility at any time.

Sit or lie down in a quiet space where you won't be disturbed. Close your eyes gently or soften your gaze if you prefer to keep them open. Take a few deep breaths, inhaling slowly and completely, exhaling fully, and releasing any tension. Bring your awareness to your body. Notice any physical sensations. Is there tightness in your shoulders? Wiggle your toes and fingers, feeling the connection between your mind and body.

Now, imagine yourself standing on the bank of a flowing river. The water represents the constant change in life. Notice the current, ever-moving, yet the riverbed itself remains steady. This is the power of adaptability, remaining grounded while embracing the flow. As you watch the river, acknowledge any resistance you feel to change. Is it fear of the unknown? A clinging to the past? See these emotions as wispy clouds drifting by in the sky. You can observe them without being swept away.

Bring your awareness back to your breath. Feel the coolness of the inhale and the warmth of the exhale. This is your anchor, your source of calm amidst the changing current. Now, imagine yourself stepping into the river. Feel the water swirling around your legs, but you are not swept away. You bend and move with the current, finding balance and ease. See yourself riding the waves of change, learning, and growing with each new experience. Notice the beauty and opportunities that unfold as you become more adaptable.

Gently step back onto the riverbank. Feel the solid ground beneath your feet. You are changed, but you are also strong and resilient. You carry the lessons learned from the flowing river within you. Take a few deep breaths and wiggle your fingers and toes again. When you feel ready, gently open your eyes. Carry the feelings of calm acceptance and adaptability with you throughout your day.

You can repeat this meditation as many times and as often as you want to. By cultivating a mindset that's open to change, you are one step closer to having it all. In the next chapter, we'll look at the importance of taking care of yourself, both mentally and physically, so get ready for some TLC!

Chapter 6:

Impact on Your Mental and Physical Health

Self-care is not a waste of time; self-care makes your use of time more sustainable.

–Jackie Viramontez

You know that popular saying, "I'll sleep when I'm dead"? Well, that was my motto for a very long time. Sleep just wasn't productive enough, in my opinion, so I kept it to a minimum. For over a decade, I functioned on four to five hours of sleep a night. I would get into bed, fall asleep immediately, and wake up after a couple of hours, ready to tackle my never-ending to-do list. If I went to bed and didn't fall asleep within minutes, I saw it as a sign that I wasn't tired, so I would get up and do something productive. I was proud of my efficient sleep schedule until I got some serious health issues; my lips and hands started going numb, almost like having a seizure. Upon meeting with a neurologist, I learned that it should take about 30 minutes to fall asleep when you get into bed. If it's less than that, you're over-tired, and it's not very healthy for you. While I thought I was being efficient, I was actually just completely sleep-deprived.

My neurologist signed me up for a sleep study, and in the study, I fell asleep within 30 seconds of closing my eyes. He said that if I didn't immediately start getting more sleep on a daily basis, I would have some serious health issues. With this major wake-up call, I decided to make some changes in my life. You might think that you don't have time to take care of your health, but if not now, when? How will you take care of all the other aspects of your life if you're not willing to take care of your physical and mental health? In this chapter, we'll explore the importance of taking care of your mental and physical health and how that can actually lead to finding a better balance.

The Interplay of Work and Health

Work and health are like two sides of the same coin. A fulfilling and balanced work environment can contribute to positive mental and physical well-being. It can provide a sense of purpose, social connection, and financial security, all of which are important for overall health. However, work can also become a source of stress, exhaustion, and unhealthy habits. Long hours, demanding workloads, and poor work-life balance can negatively impact mental health, leading to anxiety, depression, and burnout. This stress can then manifest in physical problems like weakened immunity, heart issues, and sleep disturbances. The key is finding that healthy balance where work supports your well-being.

When work depletes one's well-being, it takes a physical and mental toll. That's not surprising, as the physical and mental aspects of well-being are connected. Our mental and physical health are not separate entities but rather two sides of the same coin, intricately interwoven. When one suffers, the other feels the strain. Chronic stress, for example, which is a common outcome of work-life imbalance, can wreak havoc on our physical well-being. It weakens the immune system, making us more susceptible to illness. It can elevate blood pressure and cholesterol, increasing the risk of heart disease. Conversely, physical health issues like chronic pain or a debilitating illness can take a toll on our mental state, leading to anxiety or depression (National Institute of Mental Health, 2021).

This two-way street applies in more subtle ways. A healthy diet fuels not only our bodies but also our brains, impacting mood, focus, and cognitive function. Regular exercise improves not just physical fitness but also reduces stress hormones and promotes better sleep, both of which are crucial for mental well-being. In essence, taking care of one aspect of our health automatically benefits the other. By prioritizing a healthy lifestyle with good nutrition, exercise, and stress management, we invest in both our mental and physical well-being, creating a strong foundation for overall health and happiness.

That's why it's so important to take care of both the physical and mental aspects of your health. Achieving true vitality goes beyond just feeling physically strong or having a clear head. It's about nurturing a state of wholeness, where both your mental and physical well-being are addressed and flourish together. This comprehensive approach to wellness creates a synergy for success. A healthy mind supports a healthy body and vice versa, which is why the rest of this chapter will be devoted to looking at ways that you can prioritize your physical health if that's the area of lack or prioritize your mental health if that's the area of concern. If both need attention, this is a great place to start as you identify one or two things to improve on in both areas.

Prioritizing Physical Health

Our physical body is the foundation for everything we do. Just like a strong house needs a solid base, taking care of your body allows you to move through life with energy and resilience. When you prioritize your physical well-being, you'll have the stamina to tackle daily tasks, the strength to recover from setbacks, and the physical capacity to enjoy your favorite activities. Here are some practical ways to weave physical well-being into the fabric of your day-to-day life:

- **Fuel your body for performance:** Think of food as fuel for your body. Focus on a balanced diet rich in fruits, vegetables, and whole grains to provide your body with the essential nutrients it needs to thrive. Don't skimp on healthy fats and lean proteins, which are crucial for building and repairing tissues (Ferreira, 2018).

- **Move your body regularly:** Find an activity you enjoy, whether it's a brisk walk, a dance class, or a yoga session. Aim for at least 30 minutes of moderate-intensity exercise most days of the week (*Physical Activity*, 2018). If you're new to exercise, start gradually and increase the duration and intensity as your fitness improves. Even small bursts of activity throughout the day can make a difference. Take the stairs instead of the elevator, park farther away from your destination, or do some bodyweight exercises during your lunch break. Even a short five-minute walk can be a great place to start.

- **Prioritize quality sleep:** Aim for seven to eight hours of quality sleep each night. Establish a regular sleep schedule and create a relaxing bedtime routine to wind down before sleep. This could include taking a warm bath or shower, reading a book, or practicing relaxation techniques like deep breathing or meditation. You can also eliminate light from your room so that you stay asleep longer. A consistent sleep schedule helps regulate your body's natural sleep-wake cycle, ensuring you wake up feeling refreshed and energized (Suni, 2023).

- **Stay hydrated:** Water is essential for every bodily function, from regulating body temperature to flushing toxins. Drink plenty of water throughout the day to keep your body functioning optimally. Aim for around eight glasses of water daily. You can also incorporate hydrating fruits and vegetables like watermelon, cucumber, and celery into your diet, as well as teas and coffee (Leech, 2020).

- **Listen to your body:** Your body is constantly communicating with you. Pay attention to its signals. If you're feeling tired, take a break. If you're experiencing pain, don't ignore it. Pushing yourself too hard can lead to injury and hinder your progress. Learn to recognize your body's limits and adjust your activity level accordingly. Prioritize getting enough rest and schedule regular check-ups with your doctor to maintain optimal health (Mansour, 2019). Even just taking a few minutes to sit, reflect, and breathe throughout the day allows your body to relax and recharge.

By incorporating these simple strategies into your daily life, you can make significant strides toward improving your physical well-being and creating a strong foundation for overall health and happiness. Remember, consistency is key. Small changes, consistently applied, can lead to big improvements in your physical health and energy levels.

Prioritizing Mental Health

Just as your body is the foundation for physical actions, your mind is the command center for your thoughts, emotions, and overall well-being. Taking care of your mental health allows you to manage stress effectively, navigate challenges with a clear head, and experience a sense of joy and fulfillment in life. Here are some strategies you can use to prioritize your mental well-being on a daily basis:

- **Practice mindfulness:** Mindfulness involves focusing your attention on the present moment. Techniques like meditation or deep breathing can help quiet the mind, reduce stress, and improve emotional regulation. Many free guided meditations are available online or through apps, making it easy to incorporate mindfulness into your daily routine. Even a few minutes of mindful breathing can make a big difference (Robinson et al., 2019).

- **Challenge negative thoughts:** Our brains can sometimes get stuck in negative thought patterns, especially when tired. Actively challenge these thoughts by reframing them in a more positive light. For instance, instead of thinking, "I'm going to fail this presentation," reframe it as "I'm well-prepared, and I'm going to do my best." Cognitive Behavioral Therapy (CBT) is a form of therapy that can teach you practical tools for challenging negative thought patterns. Many self-help books and online resources are available on CBT (Cherry, 2023).

- **Connect with others:** Social connection is vital for mental health. Nurture your relationships with loved ones, build a strong support network, and don't be afraid to ask for help when you need it. Make regular plans to connect with friends and family, either in person or virtually. Join a club or group activity that interests you; this is a great way to meet new people who share your passions (CDC, 2023).

- **Make time for activities you enjoy:** Schedule time for activities that bring you joy and relaxation, whether it's reading, spending time in nature, listening to music, or pursuing a hobby. Engaging in activities you enjoy helps reduce stress hormones and promotes feelings of happiness and fulfillment. Experiment with different activities to find what works best for you (National Institute of Mental Health, 2022).

By incorporating these practices into your daily routine, you can cultivate a strong mental foundation that fosters emotional resilience, clarity, and a sense of well-being that enriches every aspect of your life. Remember, taking care of your mental health is just as important as taking care of your physical health. Don't wait until you're struggling to prioritize your mental well-being. Make it a part of your daily self-care routine, and you'll reap the benefits for years to come.

As you can see, it's essential to take care of your mental and physical health if you want to achieve fullness in your life and unlock all your potential.

Chapter Activity and Reflection Moment

This self-assessment is a tool to gain a general understanding of your current physical and mental well-being. It is not a diagnostic tool and cannot replace professional medical advice. If you have any concerns about your health, please consult a doctor or licensed therapist. Please rate each statement on a scale of 1 (Never) to 5 (Always) based on your experience in the past two weeks. There are no right or wrong answers here, so use this time to be honest with yourself.

Physical Health

1. I feel energized and have the stamina to complete my daily tasks.

2. I am able to sleep soundly and wake up feeling refreshed most mornings.

3. I experience minimal aches, pains, or stiffness throughout the day.

4. I am satisfied with my current diet and eating habits.

5. I engage in some form of physical activity most days of the week.

Mental Health

1. I feel generally optimistic and hopeful about the future.

2. I am able to manage stress in a healthy way.

3. I experience few feelings of anxiety or worry throughout the day.

4. I am able to focus and concentrate on tasks without feeling easily distracted.

5. I feel a sense of enjoyment and satisfaction in most aspects of my life.

Scoring

Once you've rated each statement, add up your scores for both the Physical Health and Mental Health sections separately.

- **Physical Health**

    o 16-25: You show signs of physically good health.

    o 11-15: You should consider incorporating more physical activity or improving your diet.

- 10 or below: There may be areas that you need to improve on. Consult your doctor for a personalized health assessment.

- **Mental Health**

    - 16-25: You show signs of generally good mental health.

    - 11-15: You might be experiencing some mild stress or low mood. Consider relaxation techniques or talking to a trusted friend or therapist.

    - 10 or below: You may need to improve in certain areas. Talking to a therapist can be a great first step to improving your mental well-being.

After completing this activity, you should have a good idea of your mental and physical health and priorities.

In the next chapter, we'll explore how your work-life balance might change over the seasons of your life. Remember, it's normal for your priorities to change as you grow and experience different seasons of your life.

Chapter 7:

Work-Life Balance Across Different Life Stages

> *Achieving work-life balance is a never-ending journey, and your needs will change over time. The key is to make time for what you love and follow your passions relentlessly.* –Chris Guillebeau

As we grow and evolve, we enter different phases of our lives. While all of our phases are unique, most of us will eventually enter similar phases as we age but perhaps at different times in our lives. It all depends on the life that we choose for ourselves. For example, you can't compare the work-life balance of a bachelor who just received his first promotion and is hustling for another with that of a middle-aged father whose youngest child just left for college. Their work-life balance will most likely look completely different. While the young and upcoming businesswoman might spend her weekends working overtime for some extra cash, the new mom of two might take Friday off from work to spend more quality time with the family.

Here's the beauty of it all: It's totally normal. The work-life balance you're creating now doesn't have to stay like this for the rest of your life. Every season requires change and adaptation as you grow into a different version of yourself. In this chapter, we'll discuss how work-life balance might change over various stages of your life. We'll start by looking at what work-life balance might look like in your early career and professional development, then how it might adapt as you enter parenting and caregiving responsibilities, and finally, we'll explore work-life balance as you become an empty nester or are starting to consider retirement. Let's begin with the early career as we explore an example of work-life balance.

Early Career and Professional Development

Early careers are a whirlwind of learning and adaptation. Just out of college, you probably work a lot of overtime and most likely don't have kids or a spouse yet. That means you have the time to work overtime while still having time for yourself. You can travel more, exercise regularly, and have time to spend with your friends. During this season, you are probably hungry for promotions, so push hard while you can. You might experience a few challenges during this season, though.

One of the biggest challenges is building a strong skill set. While academic knowledge provides a foundation, real-world experience is crucial. This can lead to feelings of inadequacy as individuals navigate new tasks and responsibilities. This is also an opportunity to be a fast learner, eager to take on new projects and absorb knowledge from mentors and colleagues. Another challenge is establishing a professional network. Building connections with peers and industry professionals opens doors to future opportunities and provides valuable advice and support. However, networking events and informational interviews can feel daunting, especially for introverts.

The final hurdle is work-life integration. The pressure to prove oneself can lead to long hours and neglect of personal needs. The key is to find an approach that works. This might involve setting boundaries, communicating openly with employers about flexibility, and learning to prioritize tasks effectively. While these challenges can be significant, the early stages of a career also offer immense opportunities. It's a time to experiment, develop a strong foundation, and build a network that will be a springboard for future success. But work-life balance is essential, even at the beginning of your career. At the beginning of your career, the drive to succeed can be a double-edged sword. You might want to work overtime, ignore your boundaries, and take on more tasks than is possible because you want to climb the ladder of success. But without the rest, personal time, and human connection, you might get burnout very early on in your career.

Juggling ambition with well-being in your early career requires intentionality, but it's not impossible. With the right strategies, you can find balance from the moment you begin a new job.

Long story short, it's essential that you remember the long-term plan. I once heard someone describe work-life balance as juggling. Some balls are made of glass, while others will bounce back up when you drop them. As a young professional, you might not have many glass balls, so it's okay to push a bit more, take professional risks, and chase your dreams boldly. But don't drop the balls that can shatter, such as family.

Parenting and Caregiving Responsibilities

Continuing with the juggling analogy, as you enter a parenting phase of your life, major glass balls get added to your juggling routine, which means that you might have to drop a few other balls in order to catch the glass balls you're protecting. You might decline a work trip because it's your child's birthday, or perhaps you might cancel your coffee appointment with a friend because your child needs to go to the doctor. That's okay. It's normal for your work-life balance to drastically change. In fact, if it doesn't change, you'll probably be in trouble. You can't raise a family and still work like you did when you were single; it simply won't work, and you'll constantly feel like you're letting your family down. But that doesn't mean that work has no place in your life during this phase or that you're not allowed to still be driven and ambitious. It might just look a little different than what it used to.

Part of why your work-life balance will change so dramatically is due to a change in your priorities. Gone are the long hours spent conquering inboxes and climbing the corporate ladder. Evenings and weekends become precious real estate for bedtime stories, school plays, and the never-ending cycle of laundry. The challenges that accompany this shift are unique and significant. Juggling childcare arrangements, navigating the ever-changing nap schedules of tiny dictators, and simply meeting the constant physical and emotional demands of tiny humans require an Olympic-level blend of flexibility and adaptability. Sleep becomes a luxury, replaced by the comforting (but often sleep-depriving) weight of a warm body curled up next to you.

However, amongst the delightful chaos of spilled juice boxes and bedtime battles, spending quality time with your children is an irreplaceable investment. These early years are the fertile ground where the seeds of strong bonds and healthy development are sown. Reading silly bedtime stories, building elaborate block towers, and simply being present for those first wobbly steps—these seemingly small moments hold immense power. They foster a sense of security and love that lays the foundation for a happy and fulfilling life for your child. This doesn't mean your ambition has to vanish entirely; it simply needs to evolve and adapt to this new chapter. You might find yourself setting smaller, more achievable goals in the short term. Perhaps you prioritize professional development opportunities that offer flexibility, allowing you to stay sharp while remaining present for your family. Technologies like telecommuting, compressed workweeks, or even exploring part-time arrangements can become your allies in this new work-life equation.

Ultimately, achieving work-life balance with children isn't about maintaining the same pace you had before parenthood. It's about embracing a new kind of drive, one fueled by the desire to be both a successful professional and a present, loving parent. It's about finding creative solutions, leveraging support systems, and carving out dedicated time for both your career and your family. It's about recognizing that fulfillment can come in many forms and that the joy of watching your child blossom can be its own powerful motivator.

Something similar might occur as you get older and you have to take care of your parents. When your parents can no longer take care of themselves, that caregiving responsibility will be added to your plate and threaten to throw the balance out of order. When this happens, you will have to change some priorities to create space in your day and routine to be a caregiver. Between unexpected appointments, managing medications, and helping with daily tasks, your time will get stretched thin. This can lead to working late or coming in early to catch up, leaving less time for relaxation and personal needs. Or perhaps it will require you to take a step back from your career and work fewer hours than you did before.

Remember that you don't have to do everything on your own. If possible, you can hire help to share in the responsibility of caregiving. Or, you can delegate certain tasks to other family members if they are around. A friend of mine converted a section of her home into a small flatlet for her parents when they could no longer live on their own. She quickly realized that she didn't have time to do all the things she used to, so she brainstormed ideas on how to balance her time. Her teenage daughter offered to step up and take on the task of helping her grandmother get dressed every morning, which created space for my friend to still get her morning exercise and meditation in before work. They also realized that her father was becoming a little restless now that he lived with his daughter, so he took on the gardening responsibilities, opening time for my friend over the weekend to spend quality time with her family. It might not be easy, but with a few shifts, it's possible to still remain balanced.

Empty Nesters and Retirement

One of the final phases that you will enter is one of an empty nester or retirement. The empty nest ushers in a significant shift in work-life balance. The once relentless rhythm of school schedules, carpool duties, and endless laundry baskets gives way to a newfound freedom and quiet, or perhaps a shift in roles as you begin to take care of your aging parents. This transition can be exhilarating yet disorienting. For many, their professional and parental identities have been central pillars for decades. Now, with children venturing out on their own journeys, it's time to redefine purpose and explore possibilities beyond the familiar roles. The initial challenge lies in navigating these shifting priorities. Retirement might be on the horizon, or perhaps a phased approach is desired. This is an opportune moment to re-evaluate career goals, consider scaling back to part-time work, pursuing a passion project that was long put on hold, or even embarking on a complete career change. Or, you may go back to working longer hours or traveling more, like in the early days of your career.

The key lies in rediscovering your personal identity outside of work and parenting. What were your passions before the demands of family life took center stage? Perhaps it's rekindling a love for travel, delving into creative pursuits like writing or painting, or volunteering your time to a cause you care about. Reconnecting with old friends, joining social groups, or taking up a new hobby are all excellent ways to build a fulfilling life outside of traditional work structures. This journey of self-discovery requires intentionality. Schedule time for exploration, just as you would a work meeting. Take a class, attend a workshop, or join a club focused on your interests. Don't be afraid to experiment and try new things; this is the time to embrace possibilities without the constraints of a packed schedule.

Remember, your purpose and value extend far beyond your career and parenting roles. You are a wealth of experience, wisdom, and untapped potential. Embrace the freedom of the empty nest as an opportunity to redefine yourself, reconnect with your passions, and build a fulfilling future centered on your own unique desires and aspirations. This is the perfect phase to view your own personal desires and needs as the glass ball that shouldn't be dropped.

As you can see, each of the three phases requires something else from you, and that's why your work-life balance should adjust accordingly. Having it all is possible in every stage of your life, but you need to know what that means to you. I have shared examples of traditional roles in life; however, these tips apply to any lifestyle you create. Everyone struggles with balance.

A good friend of mine always knew that she wanted a child-free life. But her work-life still changed dramatically as she got older, and she struggled with work-life balance. She wanted to spend more time traveling than working. She started focusing more on her priorities with her close friends and family. Now, she never misses a birthday celebration and always puts in effort to see her family and friends. Over time, her priorities and values changed, so she adjusted her life.

Chapter Activity and Reflection Moment

As we've learned already, our lives unfold in seasons, each with its own unique demands and opportunities. Finding work-life balance is an ongoing journey, requiring adjustments as we navigate these changing seasons. This exercise will help you evaluate your current stage and identify areas where your work-life balance might need tweaking.

Reflect on Your Life Stage

Consider where you are in life. Are you a young professional building a career? Perhaps you're in the throes of parenthood, or maybe you're approaching the empty nest or retirement. Briefly describe your current life stage and the key roles and responsibilities that come with it.

- Are you okay emotionally and professionally with where you are in your life and career?

- If you said no, what do you need to adjust to be satisfied with your current status?

- Can you implement these changes immediately? If not, what can you do?

Now that we've briefly touched on the obstacles in each stage of life, it's time to also consider the major obstacles preventing balance in our lives. That's what's next in Chapter 8: Overcoming Common Balance Obstacles.

Chapter 8:

Overcoming Common Balance Obstacles

Striving for excellence motivates you; striving for perfection is demoralizing. – Harriet Braiker

Many obstacles can prevent work-life balance. That's why the thought of a healthy work-life balance has become a bit of an elusive goal for many, not a reality that they can strive toward. It can quickly feel like you're at the circus, carefully trying to balance everything while walking on a tightrope, and then the tightrope is on fire, and there is no net beneath you. But what would happen if we became aware of these obstacles? If we knew the tightrope was going to be set on fire, we'd be able to pack a fire extinguisher, right? That's the beauty of understanding the obstacles in your way of work-life balance: It creates the opportunity for you to overcome them.

In this chapter, we'll look at three of the main culprits that prevent us from achieving work-life balance: perfection, fear, and pressure. Join me as we explore each of these in more detail and find ways to overcome each accordingly. You might be surprised to learn that some of these techniques simply involve loving yourself and giving yourself some grace to mess up and put down some balls every now and then. Let's get right to it, starting with the biggest culprit in my life: perfectionism.

Conquering Perfectionism

Perfectionism is a personality trait that centers around setting very high standards for yourself and others and being very critical of anything that falls short of those standards. According to Merriam-Webster (2019), perfectionism is "a disposition to regard anything short of perfection as unacceptable." In many ways, being a perfectionist is celebrated in our modern society, but it's something that can stop you from achieving rest and building relationships, even though it can also lead to achievement. There are different types of perfectionists, such as those who are very critical of themselves but not others or those who have a strong urge and need for control at all times. Regardless of the type of perfectionism, it can build a wall between you and your work-life balance.

Perfectionism acts like a vise, squeezing the potential for a healthy work-life balance out of existence. Driven by a relentless pursuit of flawlessness, perfectionists set impossibly high standards for themselves, both in the quality of their work and the efficiency with which they complete it (Curran & Hill, 2018). This translates into an ingrained sense of needing to overwork. They become tethered to their tasks, staying late at the office, neglecting breaks, and constantly feeling the pressure to be "on." Even outside of work hours, their minds stay tethered to unfinished tasks or anxieties about potential shortcomings.

The fear of imperfection is another hurdle thrown up by perfectionism. The very thought of making a mistake or delivering anything less than a flawless product can trigger intense anxiety. This fear can manifest as difficulty in delegating tasks, as perfectionists often struggle to trust others to meet their exacting standards (*What Is Perfectionism*, n.d.). It can also make it nearly impossible to truly switch off from work mode, as their minds stay preoccupied with the potential for errors or missed opportunities. This constant pressure creates a breeding ground for burnout, exhaustion, and resentment. Over time, these negative emotions can bleed into personal lives, straining relationships and hindering relaxation, the very things a healthy work-life balance is designed to nurture.

Overcoming Perfectionism

As you can see, perfectionism can become a relentless taskmaster, squeezing the joy out of both work and personal life. But there are ways to break free and cultivate a healthier outlook. Firstly, you need to challenge yourself to set goals that are realistic and not rooted in perfection. Making use of SMART goals is a great way to make this change in perspective. These goals also provide a clear roadmap to success, replacing unrealistic expectations with attainable benchmarks if you are really mindful of your expectations.

The second way to overcome perfection is to reframe mistakes. Instead of viewing them as failures, see them as stepping stones. Embrace the opportunity to learn and grow from them instead of seeing it as the end of the world. This growth mindset allows you to bounce back from setbacks with resilience. Another way to overcome perfection is by cultivating self-compression. It's crucial that you begin to treat yourself the way that you treat the people you love: with kindness and understanding. Instead of trying to be perfect, take a moment to acknowledge your efforts and celebrate the progress you've made so far, no matter how small or seemingly insignificant.

Another way to manage perfectionistic thoughts and behaviors is to use cognitive restructuring. Cognitive restructuring is a technique for deconstructing unhelpful thoughts and rebuilding them in a more balanced and accurate way (Stanborough, 2020). By using cognitive restructuring, you can challenge the critical inner voice in you by questioning its accuracy and replacing negative self-talk with more realistic and encouraging statements. Additionally, mindfulness practices can be powerful allies in overcoming perfectionism. Techniques like meditation and deep breathing can help you to become aware of your perfectionist anxieties in the moment, allowing you to choose a more balanced response instead.

For example, let's say you are overloaded with work, and you are tempted to work late to make sure that everything gets done and is perfect for the next day. However, your child just came home from summer camp, and you haven't really spoken to your spouse the whole week because they were on a business trip. You really want to go home, but you have this sinking feeling that if you don't work late, you're just being lazy and not being a good worker. At that moment, you can choose to challenge that thought and ask yourself if you really are a lazy person. What does the evidence say? Are you lazy? By looking at all your accomplishments, the hours you put in, and your dedication to your career, you can choose to go home and leave work behind, knowing that you're not being lazy by leaving to spend time with family.

Managing Fear of Failure

The second culprit that might be preventing us from achieving a work-life balance is the fear of failure. The fear of failure can cast a long shadow over achieving a healthy work-life balance, and its roots often lie in a deep-seated belief that our self-worth is tied to our achievements (Tommey, 2023). This can manifest in avoidance behaviors, where individuals procrastinate on important tasks or shy away from taking on new challenges for fear of falling short. This not only hinders professional growth but also creates a backlog of work that bleeds into personal time, fueling the cycle of anxiety.

Furthermore, the fear of failure breeds self-doubt (Cherry, 2021). Individuals constantly question their abilities, and their confidence erodes, making it difficult to delegate tasks or trust their own judgment. This can lead to overwork in an attempt to compensate for perceived shortcomings, leaving no room for personal pursuits or relaxation. The constant pressure and gnawing self-doubt then escalate into anxiety. The fear of making mistakes or disappointing others spirals, creating a state of hypervigilance that makes it nearly impossible to truly switch off and enjoy downtime.

This constant state of emotional strain not only impacts mental well-being but also spills over into personal relationships, ultimately creating the imbalance it seeks to avoid, which is why we should try our best to overcome this fear of failure.

Overcoming Fear of Failure

Reframing failure from a terrifying dead end to a natural stepping stone on the path to growth requires a conscious effort, but here's how we can do it. First, detach your self-worth from your accomplishments (Cherry, 2021). You need to recognize that your value as a person doesn't hinge on perfect execution. Remember, even successful people make mistakes. Take Thomas Edison, for example. He failed about 1,000 times before creating the first successful lightbulb (Shaffer, 2022). Thank goodness he didn't give up and instead focused on the effort and the lesson he learned.

Second, set achievable goals that prioritize progress over perfection. Start by breaking down large goals into smaller, manageable steps and celebrate these mini-victories along the way to boost your self-esteem and reinforce a sense of accomplishment.

Thirdly, you should begin to view setbacks as opportunities to learn and improve. Ask yourself, "What can I take away from this experience?" Analyze the situation, identify areas for improvement, and use that knowledge to refine your approach next time (Cherry, 2021).

Finally, to overcome the fear of failure, you need to embrace a growth mindset. Believe that your skills and abilities can be developed through consistent effort and learning from mistakes. This empowers you to see challenges as opportunities to expand your knowledge and become a better version of yourself. By adopting this perspective, you can navigate setbacks with resilience and transform failures into valuable lessons that pave the way for future success.

Societal Pressures

The third obstacle preventing us from achieving work-life balance is societal pressures. Societal norms and expectations can be a double-edged sword for work-life balance. Traditional gender roles, for instance, can place unequal burdens on men and women. Working mothers, especially, may face immense pressure to excel at both work and home, leading to guilt and exhaustion (Ziegler, 2020). Career pressures can further exacerbate the issue, especially in cultures that glorify long hours and hustle culture, where taking time for personal life can be seen as a sign of weakness or lack of dedication.

Social comparison adds another layer of complexity. Constant bombardment with curated online personas showcasing seemingly perfect work-life jugglers can fuel feelings of inadequacy and pressure to keep up (Manchiraju, 2024). These societal influences can have a significant negative impact on well-being, such as chronic stress from trying to meet unrealistic expectations, which can lead to burnout, anxiety, and even physical health problems. Furthermore, sacrificing personal pursuits for work can chip away at one's sense of identity and fulfillment. When passions and hobbies fall by the wayside, individuals may lose touch with what truly brings them joy and meaning in life.

Overcoming Societal Pressures

The best way to overcome societal pressures lies in creating boundaries to help you stick to your needs, values, and goals regardless of societal pressures. To do so, you first need to unplug and reflect. Take time away from the noise, including social media, work demands, and societal expectations. In Chapters 1-3, we identified your core values and what brings you joy and fulfillment. When facing societal pressures, reflect on how you are living in accordance with these values and ideals. Journaling and meditation are helpful tools for introspection.

Next, you need to identify your limits. Recognize your physical, emotional, and mental capacity. How much work can you realistically handle without burning out? How much personal time do you need to feel rejuvenated? After you've done that, communicate these boundaries to those around you, and make a note of them to remind yourself of these boundaries since we are often the first ones to break the boundaries that we set for ourselves. Reminding yourself of the boundaries and communicating them to others could involve setting work hours, politely declining extra commitments, or delegating tasks at work. Practice assertive communication, focusing on your needs while respecting others.

It's important to also ditch the comparison trap as much as possible. Unfollow unrealistic portrayals online and surround yourself with supportive people who respect your choices. Focus on your own journey and celebrate your personal wins, big or small. Finally, recognize that sometimes life happens, and you can't control it. There will be times when work demands more or personal commitments require adjustments. The key is to have a framework in place and be willing to adapt while staying true to your core values and long-term goals.

As you can see, overcoming these obstacles isn't impossible, but it will take some time to adjust and apply these strategies to your daily life. Don't give up, and remember to celebrate every step of the way. Here's another chapter activity to help you put all you've learned in this chapter into action.

Chapter Activity and Reflection Moment

This chapter has served as a powerful mirror, reflecting back the internal struggles we often face. Perfectionism, fear of failure, and societal pressures are deeply ingrained obstacles that can significantly impact our work-life balance and overall well-being. You can now take a moment to reflect by asking yourself the following questions.

1. Do I have any tendencies toward perfectionism? In which areas specifically?

2. How is perfectionism preventing me from living a happy, balanced life?

3. How has failing in the past helped me to become the person that I am today?

4. If my biggest fear of failure came true, what could I learn from it?

5. What societal pressures are keeping me from living a balanced life?

6. What boundaries can I put in place to prevent these pressures from causing me to stumble?

As you reflect on these questions, remember to show yourself grace and know that you are worth more than your accomplishments. In the next chapter, we'll explore how to maintain all that we've learned so far in the long term and how we can create a balanced culture for ourselves going forward.

Chapter 9:

Maintaining Work-Life Balance Long Term by Creating Balance Culture

When you have balance in your life, work becomes an entirely different experience. There is a passion that moves you to a whole new level of fulfillment and gratitude, and that's when you can do your best for yourself and for others. –Cara Delevingne

I don't know about you, but I'm not interested in short-term change. I don't want another "quick diet" that helps me to lose five pounds in a week. Why not? Because next week, I'll just gain it back. Short-term solutions are just that: short-term. They don't create lasting change, and that's what we're after here! So, how can we take all that we've learned on this journey and implement it for long-term change? How can we create a balance that lasts forever? This chapter is all about figuring it out.

If you are working for an employer, the way they run their business will have a massive impact on the longevity of your work-life balance. If they don't respect your work-life balance or constantly push you to do more, chances are that you'll feel pressure to work long hours and your work-life balance will be impacted. That's why part of this chapter will discuss the impact of an organization on its employees' work-life balance. If you're an employer, I suggest reading through it as a guide to help you see why you should implement a healthy work-life balance culture in your company.

Sustaining Work-Life Balance Over Time

Achieving and maintaining work-life balance is an ongoing challenge, especially over the long term, because our priorities and circumstances are constantly evolving. As we discussed in earlier chapters, we move through life stages and our priorities shift. Marriage, children, aging parents, or personal health concerns can all necessitate adjustments to our work schedules and commitment levels. All of this makes it challenging to create a work-life balance that lasts.

Furthermore, career changes or unexpected opportunities may arise, requiring us to re-evaluate how much time and energy we can dedicate to work. These transitions can create a constant push and pull between professional aspirations and personal needs, making it difficult to find that perfect equilibrium. Ultimately, maintaining work-life balance is a journey, not a destination, requiring flexibility, adaptability, and a willingness to re-evaluate our priorities as our lives unfold. Let's talk about a few strategies to sustain balance.

Strategies for Sustainable Balance

By incorporating the following strategies into your routine, you can develop a sustainable approach to work-life balance. It's important to remember that it's a continuous process, so be patient and adaptable and prioritize your well-being throughout your career journey. Here are five strategies for sustainable balance.

- **Regular self-assessment:** Schedule regular check-ins with yourself, quarterly or biannually, to assess your current balance. Ask yourself: How are my stress levels? Am I neglecting personal priorities? Is work interfering with my well-being? Are my core values the same? If so, am I living according to my values? Honest self-reflection allows you to identify areas that need adjustment before resentment or burnout sets in.

- **Goal setting with flexibility:** Set clear goals for both your professional and personal life. Ensure these goals are flexible and adaptable. Life throws curveballs, so be prepared to adjust your goals as priorities shift. For example, aiming for a promotion this year might take a backseat if you decide to go back to school. Don't forget to align your goals with your values.

- **Periodic course correction:** Don't be afraid to make adjustments as needed. If your self-assessment reveals a significant imbalance, be proactive. Talk to your manager about exploring flexible work arrangements, delegate tasks where possible, or schedule time for personal commitments without guilt. Remember, a supportive work environment is more likely to thrive when employees feel empowered to manage their workload.

- **Open communication:** Maintain open and honest communication with your manager, friends, and colleagues. Discuss your workload and be clear about your boundaries. A supportive manager will understand the need for work-life balance and may be able to offer solutions to lighten your load or adjust deadlines.

- **Protect your time:** Schedule "me-time" in your calendar, just like you would a work meeting. This dedicated time could be for exercise, hobbies, time spent with loved ones, or relaxation. Treat this time as sacrosanct and avoid filling it with work-related tasks.

Creating a Work-Life Balance Culture

Creating a work-life balance culture depends on several factors. First, we need to acknowledge the employer's responsibility if we want to have an accurate and realistic picture of how it works. Second, we need to consider the benefits of a healthy work-life culture and the side effects of an unbalanced culture. So, with all of that in mind, let's explore what it takes to create a work-life balance culture.

Employer Responsibility

While it's important that we learn to take care of our own work-life balance, some things are out of our control. That's where employer responsibility comes in and plays a significant role. Employers and organizations have a significant responsibility to promote work-life balance and foster a culture of well-being for their employees. This extends beyond simply offering benefits packages. Let's take a closer look at their key areas of influence.

Setting Clear Expectations and Workload Management

Unrealistic deadlines and unclear expectations are a recipe for stress and burnout. Employers can play a crucial role by clearly defining work parameters, setting achievable deadlines, and encouraging open communication about workloads (Williams, 2023). This allows employees to better manage their time and prioritize tasks, reducing the feeling of being overwhelmed. Employers should also provide tools and training to support work-life balance.

Promoting Flexible Work Arrangements

The ability to manage work schedules around personal commitments is a major factor in achieving work-life balance. Employers can offer flexible work options like remote work, compressed workweeks, or flex hours. This empowers employees to manage their time more effectively and reduces the pressure of being physically present in the office for extended periods (ActivTrak, 2023).

Leading by Example

A company's culture is heavily influenced by its leadership. Leaders who set the standard for respecting work-life boundaries and disconnecting after hours send a powerful message to employees. This encourages them to prioritize their well-being without fear of jeopardizing their careers. If you are the boss, reflect on how you behave. Are you leading by example or constantly jeopardizing your own work-life balance?

Offering Resources and Support

Employers can provide resources to help employees manage stress and improve their overall well-being. This could include access to Employee Assistance Programs (EAPs), on-site wellness programs, or educational workshops on topics like stress management, time management, and healthy living (Burton, 2023).

Encouraging Open Communication and Feedback

Creating a safe space for open communication about workload, stress levels, and work-life concerns is essential. Employees who feel comfortable voicing their needs and frustrations are more likely to feel supported and valued by their employers (*Employee Voice*, 2024).

Celebrating and Rewarding Well-Being

Recognition goes a long way. Employers can actively acknowledge and reward employees who prioritize well-being by taking breaks, utilizing flexible work arrangements, and maintaining healthy boundaries. This reinforces positive behaviors and encourages others to follow suit (Turner, 2023).

By taking a proactive approach to promoting work-life balance and fostering a culture of well-being, employers can create a work environment where employees feel valued, engaged, and productive. This translates into a happier, healthier workforce, reduced turnover rates, and, ultimately, a more successful organization.

Benefits of a Balanced Workplace

A balanced workplace, where work demands and personal lives coexist harmoniously, fosters a multitude of benefits for both companies and employees. One of the most significant advantages is a surge in productivity. When employees feel well-rested and have time to recharge outside of work, they return with renewed focus and energy. This translates into sharper minds, better decision-making, and a greater capacity to tackle challenges (Kalev & Dobbin, 2022). Furthermore, a balanced work environment fosters employee satisfaction. Feeling valued and supported by an employer who respects their personal time leads to happier and more engaged workers. This satisfaction fuels motivation and a genuine desire to contribute to the company's success.

Finally, a balanced workplace plays a crucial role in employee retention. By prioritizing well-being and offering flexible work arrangements, companies create an environment where employees feel valued and are less likely to seek opportunities elsewhere. This not only saves businesses the time and money associated with recruitment and training but also allows them to retain the knowledge, experience, and institutional memory embodied by their workforce (Kalev & Dobbin, 2022). In other words, a balanced workplace is a win-win situation, creating a more productive, satisfied, and loyal workforce that propels the organization toward long-term success.

Side Effects of Unbalanced Work-Life Culture

While the benefits of a healthy work-life culture are evident, the opposite is also true. When a company lacks a healthy culture, it will surely experience serious side effects, and it goes beyond just having happy employees. In fact, it can actually cost you dearly as an organization when you don't have a balanced work-life culture. While there are many side effects, I want to briefly highlight the ten most common side effects of an unbalanced work-life culture:

- **High turnover rates:** An unrelenting workload and constant pressure can quickly erode employee morale. Feeling burnt out and like their personal lives are neglected, employees seek greener pastures (Brett, 2014). This revolving door of new hires disrupts workflows, drains resources spent on recruitment and onboarding, and hinders the development of a cohesive team environment.

- **Decreased employee engagement:** Imagine a talented team constantly stressed and overworked. Disengaged employees become passive participants, simply going through the motions to fulfill their basic duties. They lack the motivation and focus to bring their creativity and problem-solving skills to the table, ultimately hindering innovation and overall productivity (Clifton, 2023).

- **Negative impact on organizational culture:** A company culture that prioritizes work above all else breeds resentment and cynicism among employees. This negativity permeates the work environment, impacting communication and collaboration. Employees become hesitant to share ideas or offer help, fostering a culture of isolation and hindering the team spirit necessary for success (Glassdoor, 2019).

- **Loss of top talent:** Your high performers are valuable assets, and they know it. If they feel overworked and undervalued, they'll be actively looking for opportunities elsewhere (Griffith, 2023). Losing top talent means losing not just their skills and experience but also the institutional knowledge they've accumulated over time. This brain drain can cripple a company's ability to compete and innovate.

- **Impact on recruitment efforts:** A reputation for poor work-life balance travels fast. In today's job market, potential candidates research company culture before applying. A history of high turnover and disengaged employees is a red flag that can deter qualified individuals from even considering your company. This narrows your talent pool and makes it harder to find the right people for the job (Farmer, 2023).

- **Higher costs of recruitment and training:** The cost of constantly replacing employees is significant. The time and money spent on recruiting, onboarding, and training new people can quickly add up (Charaba, 2021). This constant churn disrupts workflows and reduces overall productivity as new hires take time to get up to speed.

- **Decreased productivity:** Exhausted and disengaged employees are demonstrably less productive. They make more mistakes due to carelessness, take longer to complete tasks, and lack the energy and focus to perform at their best. This decline in individual productivity can significantly impact a company's bottom line (Postelnyak, 2022).

- **Negative impact on health and well-being:** An unbalanced work culture can lead to employee burnout, chronic stress, and even physical health problems such as heart disease and high blood pressure. This can create a vicious cycle of absenteeism and decreased productivity as employees struggle to cope with the mental and physical toll (De Hert, 2020).

- **Higher absenteeism rates:** Employees who are stressed and burnt out are more likely to call in sick, impacting team schedules and overall workflow. This increased absenteeism can put additional strain on remaining team members who have to pick up the slack, further escalating stress levels and potentially leading to a domino effect of burnout (*Work-Related Stress*, 2012).

- **Impact on employee loyalty:** When employees feel like their well-being and personal lives are an afterthought, they're less likely to be loyal to the company (Beranek, 2023). They won't go the extra mile and may be more receptive to offers from competitors who prioritize a healthy work-life balance. This lack of loyalty can hinder a company's ability to retain its best talent and build a strong, committed workforce.

As we can see, a healthy work-life balance is essential for employee well-being, productivity, and overall satisfaction. So, let's take a look at a chapter activity that will help us examine our team's or organization's current work-life culture and brainstorm ways to improve it.

Chapter Activity and Reflection Moment

Take some time to consider the following questions.

- How well does your team/organization currently promote work-life balance?

- Are there instances where work demands seem to outweigh personal time?

- Do employees feel comfortable taking breaks, using vacation days, or leaving on time?

- Are there any existing programs or initiatives that support work-life balance?

As you reflect on these answers, be honest with yourself and really ask whether the organization you're currently working for is good for your health and respect your work-life balance goals. If the answer is no, brainstorm ways to improve the culture or perhaps ways to get out of the situation you're in and move to another organization.

In the next (and final) chapter, we'll discuss technology and how it doesn't have to contribute to an unhealthy work-life balance but perhaps help with the balancing. Get ready to utilize those devices and find true balance!

Chapter 10:

Work-Life Balance in the Digital Age—Using Technology to Your Advantage

Technology is a useful servant but a dangerous master. –Christian Lous Lange

Many adults fear technology. They're so scared of AI taking over the world and leaving them without a job that they fail to recognize how it can be used for good. Others don't fear technology, but they villainize it, placing all the blame on technology for things that go wrong in their lives. Struggling in school? It must be because you're always on your phone. Struggling with intense back pain? It's because you just lay on the couch and watch TV, of course! Then you also get the people who worship technology and can't go a day without it. I believe somewhere in the middle, there is a healthy balance that we should find and utilize.

Here's the thing: Technology can make your life much easier, but it can also be a massive source of distraction. Personally, I love technology, and I don't know what I would do without our Alexa at home. She turns on the lights when it's time to get up in the morning, she plays thunderstorm sounds when I can't sleep, and in the mornings, she tells me the weather so that I know what to wear. She also keeps track of the things on my wish list and alerts me when they're on sale. Having an Alexa at home has been a game-changer. Did I shut the garage when I left this morning? Did I set the alarm? Is the house okay with the big storm going on? Has my package arrived at the front door yet? All of these questions Alexa can answer for me, allowing me to focus on my work or enjoy the holiday with my family without worries. It creates time for me to spend on the things that truly matter, allowing me to cultivate a healthy work-life balance.

In this chapter, we'll explore how to embrace technology and find the balance so that it can help contribute to our work-life balance. Let's start by exploring the impact of technology on our daily lives.

The Impact of Technology

There's no denying the truth: Technology has woven itself into the fabric of our daily lives, fundamentally changing how we work, connect, and access information. On the positive side, it's become a communication powerhouse, allowing instant connection across continents through video calls and messaging apps. Gone are the days of waiting for letters or expensive phone calls. Information access is unprecedented—researching a topic, learning a new skill, or even getting directions can all be done with a few clicks or taps. Technology has also become a productivity champion, streamlining tasks from grocery shopping to bill paying, freeing up valuable time.

However, this constant technological presence can also be a double-edged sword. The very features that connect us can become distractions, with social media notifications and news alerts constantly vying for our attention. Multitasking with technology can actually hinder our focus, leading to shallow processing of information rather than deep comprehension. The ease of information access can also create information overload, making it difficult to discern credible sources from a sea of misinformation.

Furthermore, our reliance on technology for communication can lead to social isolation and a decline in face-to-face interaction. The ability to text or message can replace the need for in-person conversations, potentially weakening social bonds and fostering feelings of loneliness. Some common culprits include emails, social media, and constant notifications on our phones. These digital distractions not only chip away at productivity but also make it difficult to truly disconnect and recharge after work. The inability to switch off can lead to stress, burnout, and a decline in overall well-being.

That's why we need to set boundaries with our technology. We can use several strategies to create healthy boundaries. One approach is to designate specific times for checking email and social media. Instead of reacting to every notification, schedule focused periods throughout the day to address these tasks. Establishing technology-free zones, like the bedroom or dinner table, can further restrict distractions and promote mindful engagement with the present moment. Additionally, leveraging productivity tools like website blockers and notification silencers can help us regain control of our digital environment, allowing uninterrupted focus on important tasks. Ultimately, setting boundaries empowers us to use technology consciously, maximizing its benefits while safeguarding our personal time, focus, and well-being.

Let's explore specific tools and how we can use them to leverage technology for balance.

Leveraging Technology for Balance

There are so many incredible gadgets and apps out there that you can use to help you gain work-life balance. The key lies in not getting so distracted by the gadget that it's actually less productive. Now, I would like to introduce you to three technology inventions that especially help me. However, you can also do your own research and find the tech that works best for you.

The reMarkable 2 Tablet

This is a cutting-edge digital device that is designed to enhance productivity, creativity, and organization while also prompting work-life balance (reMarkable, n.d.). I love this tool since it mimics the feel of writing on real paper and pen while also providing a safeguard from traditional screens.

Here's why this tablet can be a valuable tool for promoting work-life balance (reMarkable, n.d.):

- **Reduced digital distractions:** Unlike traditional tablets, the reMarkable 2's e-ink display lacks the usual culprits of digital distraction: no email, social media, or web browsing capabilities. This allows you to concentrate on your tasks without the constant ping of notifications or the temptation to multitask.

- **Analog feel for digital tasks:** Taking notes, brainstorming ideas, or creating to-do lists on the reMarkable 2 feels more like working with pen and paper. This analog experience can be more calming and focused compared to the bright, stimulating screens of traditional tablets.

- **Organization and accessibility:** The reMarkable 2 allows you to organize your work and personal notes efficiently. With notebooks, folders, and tagging features, you can keep everything categorized and easily accessible. This eliminates the need for scattered paper notes or searching through cluttered digital files, promoting a sense of control and reducing stress.

- **Disconnection to recharge:** By encouraging a more analog approach to digital tasks, the reMarkable 2 facilitates a cleaner break from work after hours. Leaving it behind allows you to truly disconnect and recharge during personal time.

- **Mindful planning and goal setting:** The reMarkable 2's note-taking capabilities can be a powerful tool for mindful planning and goal setting. Studies suggest handwriting notes improve focus and information retention. Using the reMarkable 2 to plan your day or brainstorm ideas can lead to increased focus and productivity during work hours, freeing up personal time for relaxation.

Oura Ring

Another gadget that I love is the Oura Ring and app. This wearable device tracks key biometric data to optimize users' health and well-being. It then offers insight into sleep quality, stress levels, and the ability to make informed decisions about lifestyle (Song, 2021). Here's why the Oura ring and its companion app can be helpful tools for promoting work-life balance by leveraging technology in a way that focuses on self-awareness and personalized insights (Song, 2021).

- **Sleep tracking and optimization:** The Oura ring tracks sleep stages, heart rate variability, and other physiological markers to assess sleep quality. The app provides personalized feedback and recommendations to improve sleep hygiene, a crucial factor in work-life balance. Better sleep can lead to increased focus and energy during work hours, allowing for better task completion and potentially reducing the need for overtime.

- **Stress monitoring and management:** The Oura ring can detect physiological signs of stress, such as elevated heart rate and body temperature. The app translates this data into actionable insights, suggesting stress-management techniques like meditation or deep breathing exercises. By proactively managing stress levels, individuals can improve their overall well-being and prevent burnout, which can negatively impact work-life balance.

- **Recovery monitoring:** The Oura app analyzes data to determine an individual's recovery readiness. This information can guide decisions about workload and activity levels. By scheduling demanding tasks on days with high recovery scores, users can optimize their work performance and reduce the risk of overexertion. This can help create a clearer separation between work and personal time.

- **Activity tracking and goal Setting:** The Oura ring tracks daily activity levels and provides personalized goals to encourage a healthy lifestyle. This can motivate users to incorporate physical activity into their daily routine, which can improve mood, reduce stress, and boost overall well-being. A healthy lifestyle can improve work performance and overall well-being, contributing to a better work-life balance.

ChatGPT

ChatGPT can be a valuable asset in your quest for a healthier work-life balance. As a large language model, it can act as a powerful virtual assistant, automating tasks and streamlining your workflow (*ChatGPT for Work*, 2024). I use ChatGPT to help me plan meals for the week, generate a shopping list, write emails, and generate recommendations for me. For example, I would ask ChatGPT to provide me with five date night ideas when I'm low on inspiration but want to do something nice for my husband. Here's how this tool can help you daily.

- **Boost efficiency:** By automating tasks like data entry, summarizing information, and generating creative text formats like emails and presentations, ChatGPT can free up significant chunks of your workday. This allows you to focus on more strategic or complex tasks or simply clock out on time.

- **Prioritize effectively:** Feeling overwhelmed by your to-do list? ChatGPT can help you sort through tasks and emails, identifying the most important ones and scheduling them efficiently.

- **Set boundaries:** ChatGPT can be a virtual assistant, answering work questions after hours so you don't feel pressured to stay glued to your inbox. This allows you to maintain a clearer separation between work and personal life.

- **Find inspiration:** Feeling stuck on a project? Brainstorm with ChatGPT! It can generate new ideas and help you approach problems from fresh angles.

Overall, ChatGPT can be a time-saving and creativity-sparking tool that empowers you to get more done in less time, leaving you with more energy for personal pursuits and reducing work-related stress.

Digital Well-Being Practices

In today's hyper-connected world, cultivating digital well-being practices is essential for maintaining a healthy relationship with technology and mitigating its negative impact on work-life balance. Here are some key strategies to achieve this.

- **Mindfulness:** The first step is cultivating mindfulness around our tech use. Taking mindful pauses throughout the day to assess how you're feeling and what technology you're engaging with can be transformative. Are you mindlessly scrolling through social media, or are you using it for a specific purpose? By being present in the moment, you can make conscious choices about how you engage with technology.

- **Screen time limits:** Setting clear boundaries with technology is crucial. Utilize built-in phone features or download apps to set screen time limits for specific apps or even the entire device. Schedule designated times to check emails and social media and resist the urge to constantly check notifications. This allows for focused work periods and uninterrupted personal time.

- **Intentional tech use:** Move beyond passive consumption and cultivate intentional tech habits. Instead of aimlessly browsing, plan your online activities with specific goals in mind. Schedule time for learning new skills, connecting with loved ones online, or pursuing hobbies that involve technology. This intentional approach empowers you to use technology for specific purposes rather than letting it control your time.

By incorporating these practices, you can create a healthier relationship with technology. Mindfulness helps you make conscious choices, screen time limits establish boundaries, and intentional tech use ensures you're deriving value from your online activities. Ultimately, these digital well-being practices empower you to achieve a greater sense of balance and presence in your daily life.

Now that you have a clear picture of what a healthy relationship with tech looks like, let's explore our final chapter activity as we reflect on what we've learned.

Chapter Activity and Reflection Moment

Technology is an undeniable force in our lives, impacting everything from how we work to how we unwind. But with great power comes great responsibility (and potential for distraction!). This activity will help you assess your relationship with technology and explore ways to use it more mindfully for a healthier work-life balance.

Part 1: A Digital Detox Audit

Start by tracking your current tech usage. Grab a pen and paper or your favorite note-taking app. For the next 24 hours, track your technology usage. You can note down:

- the type of device (phone, laptop, tablet)

- the activity you were engaged in (work emails, social media, online learning)

- the duration of your usage

- the feelings you experienced after using the technology (energized, drained, anxious)

Once completed after 24 hours, take a moment to review and reflect. Look over your log. What patterns emerge? Are there specific times of day when you tend to reach for your devices more often? What types of activities leave you feeling recharged, and which ones drain your energy?

Part 2: Taming the Tech Tigers

Once you've reflected and reviewed your usage, be honest with yourself as you determine your distraction. How effective are your current strategies for managing digital distractions? Do you silence notifications? Do you have designated tech-free zones? Next, remember that technology can be a powerful tool for well-being, not just a distraction. Think about your work-life balance goals. How could you leverage technology to support them?

Part 3: Your Digital Well-Being Manifesto

Based on your audit and brainstorming, create a personalized "Digital Wellbeing Manifesto." This can be a list of actionable steps you'll take to promote a healthier relationship with technology. Here are some prompts to get you started:

- I will silence notifications during work hours and schedule dedicated times to check emails and social media.

- I will create a tech-free zone in my bedroom for a more restful sleep.

- For every hour spent mindlessly scrolling, I will dedicate 30 minutes to a technology-free activity (reading, spending time with loved ones, exercising).

- I will leverage technology to support my well-being by using apps for X (meditation, fitness tracking, learning a new language).

Remember, a healthy relationship with technology is like any other—it takes work and conscious effort. But the rewards of improved focus, reduced stress, and a better work-life balance are well worth it!

Conclusion

Having it all doesn't mean being a superwoman. It's a realistic dream, not something we should see as impossible or fictional. The problem doesn't lie in wanting it all. The problem lies in not knowing what "all" means to us. However, I hope this book has helped you identify your all and that you have a clear path forward. I can't believe we've already reached the end of our journey together, but I'm going to let you in on a secret: This isn't the end. It might be the end for the two of us together, but your journey to unlocking your full potential has just begun.

In this book, we've explored the ever-elusive concept of work-life balance. We've delved into the dangers of imbalance, the importance of self-awareness, and the multitude of strategies for creating a life that feels fulfilling and sustainable. But the truth is, work-life balance isn't a fixed destination but rather a continuous journey. It's about navigating the inevitable ebbs and flows of life, making adjustments as needed, and prioritizing your well-being throughout. After all, a balanced life isn't about achieving equal parts work and leisure every single day. It's about creating a life where all the important aspects (career, relationships, health, personal growth) have space to thrive.

The tools and strategies outlined here are your companions on this journey. Use them, adapt them, and most importantly, listen to your own unique needs. There will be days when work demands your full attention, and that's okay. But remember to schedule time for rest, rejuvenation, and the things that bring you joy. By prioritizing your well-being, both mental and physical, you'll be better equipped to handle the challenges and embrace the opportunities that life throws your way. May this book serve as a springboard for a more balanced, fulfilling, and truly vibrant life.

If you don't feel ready for a solo journey just yet, let's take a moment to reflect on how far you've come as we look at all the topics we covered on this journey:

- This book delved into the concept of work-life balance, exploring its definition, the benefits it offered, and the challenges it presented. We examined misconceptions and myths surrounding work-life balance and the consequences of neglecting it.

- We then assessed your own work-life balance. You were equipped with tools to evaluate your current situation, creating a solid foundation for your journey forward.

- Following the self-assessment, we explored strategies for achieving a balance that allowed everyone to thrive. This included practical tips, discussions of common challenges, and methods for managing stress and burnout.

- Chapter 4 focused on nurturing relationships. We acknowledged the need for both self-compassion and growth for ourselves and those around us. The importance of healthy relationships with family, friends, and colleagues was emphasized, and you were provided with tips to maintain strong connections even amidst career pursuits.

- We then shifted gears to discuss the importance of flexibility, adaptation, and embracing change. We explored strategies for finding creative solutions to life's challenges.

- Next, we revealed the impact of poor work-life balance on mental and physical health. We emphasized the importance of self-care as a foundation for achieving a fulfilling life. We also addressed cultivating meaning and healthy habits that contribute to overall satisfaction.

- Chapter 7 explored how work-life balance needs and priorities change over time, from the beginning of your career to retirement. Advice was provided for every stage, including specific considerations for parents, caregivers, empty nesters, and retirees.

- Following the discussion of life stages, we addressed common obstacles encountered on the path to true balance. Practical tips and solutions were offered to overcome these obstacles and build resilience.

- Chapter 9 focused on maintaining the work-life balance you've achieved. We discussed strategies for ongoing assessment and adaptation to ensure lasting change.

- Finally, the book concluded by exploring how technology can be leveraged to enhance work-life balance. We acknowledged the digital age and explored ways to integrate technology into daily life for the benefit of both personal and professional spheres.

As you can see, we covered a lot of ground, and do you know what that means? You're prepared. You're equipped. And you've been empowered to make the most of your life and find that delicate work-life balance that you've been craving. I trust that you've learned a great deal on this journey with me and that you are now ready to spread your wings and have it all.

If you enjoyed this book and found it helpful, please consider leaving a review so that others can find their way on their own journey as well. I can't wait to hear your success stories and see you flourish from work to life and all other areas of your being. Now, get out there and work smarter, not harder. I believe in you!

About The Author

Elizabeth Bright is a passionate advocate for positivity and happiness, dedicated to helping others find balance in their lives. With a Bachelor's and Master's degree in unrelated fields, Elizabeth's diverse educational background enriches her perspective on life and fuels her commitment to personal growth and fulfillment.

Married and a devoted mother of three daughters, Elizabeth understands the importance of juggling multiple roles while maintaining a sense of harmony. Balancing her pursuit of a Ph.D. with her roles as an executive at a prominent company, a university lecturer, and an active community volunteer, she embodies the belief that happiness is not just a destination but a way of life.

Elizabeth is also an accomplished author, known for her book "Happy Habits," which offers practical insights and strategies for cultivating joy and well-being. Her writing reflects her unwavering optimism and her belief in the transformative power of positivity.

Despite her busy schedule, Elizabeth prioritizes self-care and cherishes moments spent with family and friends. Through her own journey, she demonstrates that finding balance is not only achievable but essential for living a fulfilling and meaningful life.

With boundless enthusiasm and a genuine desire to make a difference, Elizabeth Bright continues to inspire others to embrace happiness, pursue their passions, and create their own paths to fulfillment.

References

Abrams, Z. (2023, June 1). *The science of why friendships keep us healthy.* American Psychological Association. https://www.apa.org/monitor/2023/06/cover-story-science-friendship

ActivTrak. (2023, December 22). *5 types and examples of flexible work arrangements.* ActivTrak. https://www.activtrak.com/blog/flexible-work-arrangement-examples/

American Psychological Association. (2023). *2023 work in America survey.* American Psychological Association. https://www.apa.org/pubs/reports/work-in-america/2023-workplace-health-well-being

Arun, R. (2023, February 14). *What is Trello and how to use it?* Simplilearn. https://www.simplilearn.com/tutorials/project-management-tutorial/what-is-trello

Baron, A. (2015, April 16). *A 21st century way of life: From 20th century work-life balance to lifeworking.* Adventures of LIFEaholics. https://medium.com/life-working/a-21st-century-way-of-life-from-20th-century-work-life-balance-to-lifeworking-7c29f8b13690

Beranek, C. (2023, March 10). *Council post: What does employee loyalty look like today?* Forbes. https://www.forbes.com/sites/forbestechcouncil/2023/03/30/what-does-employee-loyalty-look-like-today/?sh=60947ae63ddc

Borowiec, A. A., & Drygas, W. (2023). Work-life balance and mental and physical health among Warsaw specialists, managers and entrepreneurs. *International Journal of Environmental Research and Public Health, 20*(1), 492. https://doi.org/10.3390/ijerph20010492

Brett, J. (2014). Why people really quit their jobs. *Harvard Business Review, 92*(12), 88-95.

Burton, J. (2023, April 21). *Workplace stress: 7 ways employers can help*. MQ Mental Health. https://www.mqmentalhealth.org/workplace-stress-7-ways-employers-can-help/

Cadario, R., & Morewedge, C. K. (2022). Why do people eat the same breakfast every day? Goals and circadian rhythms of variety seeking in meals. *Appetite, 168*, 105716. https://doi.org/10.1016/j.appet.2021.105716

Caring for your mental health. (2022, December). National Institute of Mental Health. https://www.nimh.nih.gov/health/topics/caring-for-your-mental-health

Casarella, J. (2022, December 18). *Signs of a toxic person*. WebMD. https://www.webmd.com/mental-health/signs-toxic-person

CDC. (2023, March 30). *How does social connectedness affect health?* Centers for Disease Control and Prevention. https://www.cdc.gov/emotional-wellbeing/social-connectedness/affect-health.htm

Charaba, C. (2021, September 17). *Employee retention - the real cost of losing an employee*. People Keep. https://www.peoplekeep.com/blog/employee-retention-the-real-cost-of-losing-an-employee

ChatGPT for work: Tips, tricks, and top applications for enhanced productivity. (2024, January 24). Jenni. https://jenni.ai/chat-gpt/work-uses

Cherry, K. (2021, May 18). *How to deal with the fear of failure.* Verywell Mind. https://www.verywellmind.com/what-is-the-fear-of-failure-5176202

Cherry, K. (2023, November 2). *What is cognitive behavioral therapy (CBT)?* Verywell Mind. https://www.verywellmind.com/what-is-cognitive-behavior-therapy-2795747

Chronic illness and mental health: Recognizing and treating depression. (2021). National Institute of Mental Health. https://www.nimh.nih.gov/health/publications/chronic-illness-mental-health

Clifton, J. (2023). *State of the global workplace report.* Gallup. https://www.gallup.com/workplace/349484/state-of-the-global-workplace.aspx

Cline, E. (2020, August 12). Toxic influences. *Mental Health Association of East Tennessee.* https://www.mhaet.com/toxic-influences/#:~:text=In%20fact%2C%2084%25%20of%20women

Curran, T., & Hill, A. (2018, May 30). *Perfectionism is increasing, and that's not good news.* Harvard Business Review. https://hbr.org/2018/01/perfectionism-is-increasing-and-thats-not-good-news

Davachi, A. (2023, October 30). *Council post: Change is inevitable—it's time to embrace it.* Forbes. https://www.forbes.com/sites/forbesbusinesscouncil/2023/10/30/change-is-inevitable-its-time-to-embrace-it/?sh=3d5c356e58b3

De Hert, S. (2020). Burnout in healthcare workers: Prevalence, impact and preventative strategies. *Local and Regional Anesthesia, 13*(13), 171–183. https://doi.org/10.2147/lra.s240564

Deal, J. (2022, October 17). *Why "balance" is a faulty metaphor.* Center for Creative Leadership. https://www.ccl.org/articles/leading-effectively-articles/balance-is-a-faulty-metaphor/#:~:text=satisfying%20and%20productive.-,Why%20the%20Work%2DLife%20%E2%80%9CBalance%E2%80%9D%20Metaphor%20Doesn't,false%20(and%20unhelpful)%20dichotomy.

Elazab, S. (2023, April 27). *Importance of setting boundaries: How to create work-life balance.* LinkedIn. https://www.linkedin.com/pulse/importance-setting-boundaries-how-create-work-life-balance-elazab/

Eludinni, E. (2016, November 24). *Consequences of work-life imbalance.* LinkedIn. https://www.linkedin.com/pulse/consequences-work-life-imbalance-elizabeth-eludinni/

Employee Voice. (2024, February 16). CIPD. https://www.cipd.org/uk/knowledge/factsheets/voice-factsheet/

Farmer, M. (2023, April 25). *10 interview red flags that are a turn off for job candidates.* 2i Recruit. https://2irecruit.co.uk/10-interview-red-flags-that-are-a-turn-off-for-job-candidates/#:~:text=Staff%20turnover%20rates

Ferreira, M. (2018). *6 essential nutrients: What they are and why you need them.* Healthline. https://www.healthline.com/health/food-nutrition/six-essential-nutrients

54 powerful work-life balance quotes to inspire you. (n.d.). Chair Office. Retrieved April 1, 2024, from https://www.chairoffice.co.uk/blog/work-life-balance-quotes/

Getchius, J. (2019, July 5). *Lack of self-care: Consequences and tips to improve.* Psych Central. https://psychcentral.com/blog/self-care-why-is-it-so-important-why-is-it-so-hard

Glassdoor. (2019, November 25). *New survey: Company mission & culture matter more than salary.* Glassdoor. https://www.glassdoor.com/blog/mission-culture-survey/#:~:text=Glassdoor's%20Mission%20%26%20Culture%20Survey%202019,mission%20and%20purpose%20before%20applying.

Griffith, D. B. (2023). *Are you asking too much of your high performers?* Higher Ed Jobs. https://www.higheredjobs.com/Articles/articleDisplay.cfm?ID=3387

Gudhka, P. (2023, June 7). *The power of prioritizing self-care and mental health in the workplace.* LinkedIn. https://www.linkedin.com/pulse/power-prioritizing-self-care-mental-health-workplace-prachi-gudhka/

Herrity, J. (2023, February 4). *55 inspirational work-life balance quotes for motivation.* Indeed. https://www.indeed.com/career-advice/career-development/work-life-balance-quotes

Hornsby, M. (2022, February 14). *A history of remote work: From hunter gatherers to the industrial revolution to the internet to wifi - and how technology will keep us telecommuting.* Telnet. https://www.telnetww.com/blog/remote-work/a-history-of-remote-work-telecommuting/#:~:text=Early%20Life%20to%20the%20Middle

Kalev, A., & Dobbin, F. (2022, August 15). The surprising benefits of work/life support. *Harvard Business Review.* https://hbr.org/2022/09/the-surprising-benefits-of-work-life-support

Leech, J. (2020, June 30). *7 science-based health benefits of drinking enough water.* Healthline. https://www.healthline.com/nutrition/7-health-benefits-of-water

Ljungkvist, H., & Moore, M. (2023). *The challenges of achieving work-life balance in the digital age: A study of young professionals exploring the impact of new ways of working on early career adults.* https://www.diva-portal.org/smash/get/diva2:1769245/FULLTEXT02.pdf

Manchiraju, S. (2024, January 27). *Mirror, mirror on the wall: Reflecting on consumption and the quest for self-esteem.* Medium. https://medium.com/@srikantmanchiraju/mirror-mirror-on-the-wall-reflecting-on-consumption-and-the-quest-for-self-esteem-4b5019037c51

Mansour, S. (2019, September 19). *5 signs you're pushing yourself too hard in the gym.* NBC News. https://www.nbcnews.com/better/lifestyle/5-signs-you-re-working-out-too-hard-ncna1053186

Mental Health Foundation. (2023). *Top tips on building and maintaining healthy relationships.* Mental Health Foundation. https://www.mentalhealth.org.uk/our-work/public-engagement/healthy-relationships/top-tips-building-and-maintaining-healthy-relationships

Merriam-Webster. (2019). Perfectionism. In *Merriam-Webster.com dictionary.* https://www.merriam-webster.com/dictionary/perfectionism

Motion Blog. (2023, June 9). *10 benefits of work-life balance for your organization.* Use Motion. https://www.usemotion.com/blog/benefits-of-work-life-balance

Myers, C. (2017, June 20). *Deconstructing the myth of work/life balance for entrepreneurs*. Forbes. https://www.forbes.com/sites/chrismyers/2017/06/20/deconstructing-the-myth-of-worklife-balance-for-entrepreneurs/?sh=72fcb20f6eec

Physical activity - it's important. (2018). Better Health Channel. https://www.betterhealth.vic.gov.au/health/healthyliving/physical-activity-its-important

Postelnyak, M. (2022, April 21). *Calculating the cost of employee disengagement*. Contact Monkey. https://www.contactmonkey.com/blog/cost-of-employee-disengagement

reMarkable. (n.d.). *ReMarkable support web*. ReMarkable. Retrieved April 19, 2024, from https://support.remarkable.com/s/article/About-reMarkable-2#:~:text=reMarkable%202%20replaces%20your%20notebooks

Robinson, L., Segal, J., & Smith, M. (2019, May 2). *Relaxation techniques for stress relief*. Help Guide. https://www.helpguide.org/articles/stress/relaxation-techniques-for-stress-relief.htm

Shaffer, L. (2022, June 19). *You really can learn as much from failure as you do success*. Fast Company. https://www.fastcompany.com/90761446/you-really-can-learn-as-much-from-failure-as-you-do-success

Sheldon, R., & Wigmore, I. (2022, September). *What is pomodoro technique?* What Is. https://www.techtarget.com/whatis/definition/pomodoro-technique

66 technology quotes to inspire innovation. (2022, August 22). Gracious Quotes. https://graciousquotes.com/technology/

Song, V. (2021, November 22). *Oura ring generation 3 review: A relationship for the long term.* The Verge. https://www.theverge.com/22789248/oura-ring-3-review-sleep-tracker-fitness-tracker

Stanborough, R. J. (2020, February 4). *How to change negative thinking with cognitive restructuring.* Healthline. https://www.healthline.com/health/cognitive-restructuring

Suni, E. (2023, September 8). *What is circadian rhythm?* Sleep Foundation. https://www.sleepfoundation.org/circadian-rhythm

Sutler-Cohen, S. (2019, March 6). *Core values: What they are, why they matter, and how to define yours.* Medium. https://medium.com/@scoutcoaching/core-values-what-they-are-why-they-matter-and-how-to-define-yours-93164383eada

The Eisenhower matrix: How to prioritize your to-do list. (2022, October 4). Asana. https://asana.com/resources/eisenhower-matrix

The progressive era. (n.d.). The American Yawp. https://www.americanyawp.com/text/20-the-progressive-era/

Tomazevic, N., Kozjek, T., & Stare, J. (2014). The consequences of a work-family (im)balance: From the point of view of employers and employees. *International Business Research, 7*(8). https://doi.org/10.5539/ibr.v7n8p83

Tommey, M. (2023). *Overcoming the fear of failure.* Matt Tommey Mentoring. https://www.matttommeymentoring.com/fear_of_failure.html#:~:text=One%20reason%20the%20fear%20of

Turner, A. (2023, April 14). *Take a break: How employers can encourage their teams to make the most of time off.* Australia. https://employmenthero.com/blog/tips-for-encouraging-time-off/

Uniyal, M. (2023, October 13). *Value vs. effort matrix technique for prioritization.* LinkedIn. https://www.linkedin.com/pulse/value-vs-effort-matrix-technique-prioritization-uniyal-she-her-/

Venkat, S. R. (2022, May 23). *Health benefits of hobbies.* WebMD. https://www.webmd.com/balance/health-benefits-of-hobbies

Wedgwood, J. (2022, September 21). *The importance of work-life balance.* The Happiness Index. https://thehappinessindex.com/blog/importance-work-life-balance/

What is perfectionism and how do I overcome it? (n.d.). Anxiety Canada. https://www.anxietycanada.com/articles/how-to-overcome-perfectionism/#:~:text=However%2C%20adults%20with%20perfectionism%20tend

Williams, I. (2023, August 11). *The role of companies in promoting work-life balance.* UnitBirwelco. https://www.unitbirwelco.com/post/the-role-of-companies-in-promoting-work-life-balance

Wong, K., Chan, A. H. S., & Ngan, S. C. (2019). The effect of long working hours and overtime on occupational health: A meta-analysis of evidence from 1998 to 2018. *International Journal of Environmental Research and Public Health, 16*(12), 2102.

Working hours. (2013). Striking Women. https://www.striking-women.org/module/workplace-issues-past-and-present/working-hours

Work-related stress. (2012). Better Health Channel. https://www.betterhealth.vic.gov.au/health/healthyliving/work-related-stress

Ziegler, S. G. (2020, September 4). *How to let go of working-mom guilt*. Harvard Business Review. https://hbr.org/2020/09/how-to-let-go-of-working-mom-guilt#:~:text=It%20feels%20like%20a%20no

About The Author

Elizabeth Bright is a passionate advocate for positivity and happiness, dedicated to helping others find balance in their lives. With a Bachelor's and Master's degree in unrelated fields, Elizabeth's diverse educational background enriches her perspective on life and fuels her commitment to personal growth and fulfillment.

Married and a devoted mother of three daughters, Elizabeth understands the importance of juggling multiple roles while maintaining a sense of harmony. Balancing her pursuit of a Ph.D. with her roles as an executive at a prominent company, a university lecturer, and an active community volunteer, she embodies the belief that happiness is not just a destination but a way of life.

Elizabeth is also an accomplished author, known for her book "Happy Habits," which offers practical insights and strategies for cultivating joy and well-being. Her writing reflects her unwavering optimism and her belief in the transformative power of positivity.

Despite her busy schedule, Elizabeth prioritizes self-care and cherishes moments spent with family and friends. Through her own journey, she demonstrates that finding balance is not only achievable but essential for living a fulfilling and meaningful life.

With boundless enthusiasm and a genuine desire to make a difference, Elizabeth Bright continues to inspire others to embrace happiness, pursue their passions, and create their own paths to fulfillment.

www.ingramcontent.com/pod-product-compliance
Lightning Source LLC
Chambersburg PA
CBHW070247230526
45470CB00002B/504